KU-343-418

YOU,
Incorporated

Your Career Is
Your Business

Ines Temple

nb

NICHOLAS BREALEY
PUBLISHING

BOSTON • LONDON

First published in 2018 by Nicholas Brealey Publishing
An imprint of John Murray Press

An Hachette UK company

23 22 21 20 19 18   1 2 3 4 5 6 7 8 9 10

Copyright © Ines Temple, 2018

The right of Ines Temple to be identified as the Authors of the Work has been
asserted by her in accordance with the Copyright, Designs and Patents Act 1988.

All rights reserved. No part of this publication may be reproduced, stored in a
retrieval system, or transmitted, in any form or by any means without the prior
written permission of the publisher, nor be otherwise circulated in any form of
binding or cover other than that in which it is published and without a similar
condition being imposed on the subsequent purchaser.

A CIP catalogue record for this title is available from the British Library

Library of Congress Control Number: 2018946205

ISBN 978-1-47368-885-8
US eBook 978-1-47368-891-9
UK eBook ISBN 978-1-47368-893-3

Printed and bound in the United States of America.

John Murray Press policy is to use papers that are natural, renewable and
recyclable products and made from wood grown in sustainable forests.
The logging and manufacturing processes are expected to conform to the
environmental regulations of the country of origin.

John Murray Press Ltd   Nicholas Brealey Publishing
Carmelite House   Hachette Book Group
50 Victoria Embankment   53 State Street
London EC4Y 0DZ   Boston, MA 02109, USA
Tel: 020 3122 6000   Tel: (617) 263 1834

www.nbuspublishing.com

To my children:

To Diego Rafael, whose lucidity has illuminated my life since the day he was born. You have helped me see and understand what I am unable to see on my own.

To Jimena, whose extraordinary attitude inspires me to face life's difficulties with my head held high . . . and keep smiling.

To Lorena, whose sharp mind and charming nature pushes me to become a better person and always strive for the best I can be.

Also:

To my mother, who is no longer with us; she would have been very pleased with this book.

CONTENTS

CONTENTS

CONTENTS

CONTENTS

ABOUT THE AUTHOR

Ines Temple (inestemple.com)

Ines is a successful entrepreneur who operates businesses in various sectors in Peru and Chile.

Her companies, LHH Peru & Chile, are the leading career transition and talent-development organizations in both countries. Her self-storage business in Peru is the country's leading company within the industry.

She is an independent board member of several corporations and nonprofit organizations. Ines was recently president of the board of CARE Peru, the leading nonprofit humanitarian organization in Peru fighting poverty. She was vice president of the board of the American Chamber of Commerce in Peru. She was also president of the board of Peru2021, the leading organization that promotes social responsibility and of OWIT Peru, the leading organization for women in business.

In 2016 and 2017, Ines' reputation and leadership earned her recognition as one of the top 13 business leaders in Peru. She was also rated second among businesswomen leaders in 2017.

A prolific content generator, she has published over 800 articles and videos on topics such as the new world of work, personal branding, and employability. In 2016 and again in 2017, she was recognized as the No. 1 personality in the country for online presence. During the past three years, she has also been recognized as the top CEO with online presence in Peru.

She recently received the Stephen G. Harrison Star Thrower Award 2018, a prestigious Lee Hecht Harrison award given to those who contribute the most to making a difference in the lives of others.

As author of the Latin American bestseller *Usted S.A.* (*You, Incorporated: Your Career Is Your Business*) published in 2010, her book is now in its 16th edition and was second in overall sales in Peru in 2012 and again in 2014. It was first in overall sales among business books in 2013. *Usted S.A.* was still on the list of the top 10 bestsellers for several weeks in 2016 and 2017.

She has a business degree from New York University and an MBA from Adolfo Ibañez School of Management. She has completed leadership courses at various universities, Harvard, Northwestern, Georgetown, and Singularity.

Ines has three children.

ACKNOWLEDGMENTS

I would like to dedicate this book to all those who, from the first day I set out on this journey, have accompanied me on this gratifying adventure of employability, relocation, and personal branding.

Many thanks to Jimena Mendoza, Raquel Arciniega, Guido Echevarria, Fernando Zapater, Rosario Almenara, Aida Marin, Patricia Canepa, Jose de Bernardis, Monica Berger, Hortensia Casanova, Lucas Reaño, Jorge Vargas, Andres Borasino, Julissa Temoche, Priscila Apaza, and the team of directors, consultants, professionals, assistants, and support personnel at Lee Hecht Harrison Peru. I have learned something from each and every one of you and profoundly admire your dedication to service, your talent, and your enormous generosity.

And thanks to Ivette Johnson and Iris MacKenzie, whose last-minute edits to the English version of the book made it a much more natural and conversational read. This is an example of the advantage of being fluent in multiple languages!

My thanks also go out to Marie Rosso, Edgardo Loret de Mola, and Luis Gomez, who gave me many valuable comments to improve my work.

I would also like to mention Myriam Valcarcel, my assistant. I can't live without her. She has given generously of her time to act as my "right-hand woman" (and my left-hand woman, too). Myriam is a living example of employability, courage, and the strength of working women everywhere.

And I can't forget Max Hernandez, who never lost hope that these ideas would one day be published. He gave me a tremendous amount of encouragement along the way. Thanks for everything, Max!

Many thanks to my aunt Elsa Arciniega, who has always believed in me, given me her unwavering support, and been a true life example.

My heartfelt appreciation goes out to Vicky Bloch, who believed in my ability to run DBM in Peru 25 years ago and later supported my work in Chile. I have learned so much from her!

Many thanks to my mentors (although some may not be aware that I have always considered them as such), who have always been there when I needed good advice, or just their friendship.

I would also like to thank each of the executives and professionals undergoing a transition process at Lee Hecht Harrison in Peru and Chile who have helped me to move on professionally. I have learned a great deal from all of these men and women, and I admire them for their courage during their professional relocation process. Thanks to all of you!

And I can't forget all of those who have read the previous editions of the Spanish version of *You, Incorporated (Usted*

S.A.), and have provided countless comments (all of which were appreciated). Many felt that the book has contributed to making them more employable; I find this enormously satisfying, and I am very grateful for their feedback.

I will be forever grateful to Lee Hecht Harrison's clients in both countries and to their managers, who have trusted us to help them manage their employees' exit processes and subsequent relocation.

And to my dear friends in the media, thank you for helping me spread the ideas in this book. You have helped me in my personal mission to take the concepts of employability and personal marketing to every corner of the continent.

Many thanks to Ruben Silva, editor of the Spanish version of the book. He was infinitely patient during the process to complete this project, and he possesses a wonderful knack for finding the right words to express my ideas. His commitment was unwavering. And I can't forget to mention David Abanto—his help was crucial and appreciated.

My thanks also go out to Javier Arevalo, who walked me through the initial stages of creating this book. His wisdom, talent, and art helped to set many of my ideas in writing. Thanks, Javier!

This work would not have been possible without the support of the international firm of Lee Hecht Harrison and its affiliates, where we have the opportunity to passionately live our calling to raise people's employability. This company is where I learned everything I know about all of the topics discussed in this text.

And thanks to my parents, wherever they may be. Thank you for always believing in me and guiding my life with your values, example, and enormous love.

And to God, for always standing by me and unconditionally supporting me.

INTRODUCTION

My father was a good man. He was very intelligent and highly respected. Medicine was his occupation and his calling; he worked his entire life at the Worker's Hospital of Lima.

He also died there.

When I started working, I followed the model that he taught me. This model was based on the following components:

1. Work hard in school.
2. Study a lot.
3. Get good grades.
4. Find a job at a good company.
5. Make a career over a lifetime there.

My father said, "If you follow these steps, you will have a job for life."

Most people were raised with very similar career aspirations, but *a job for life* is an endangered species today. In fact, it's virtually extinct, and it's one of the many paradigms that have changed in today's professional world. To thrive, we must move quickly to change and adapt ourselves within this constantly evolving work environment.

This book moves beyond sharing why things continue to change so dramatically in the job market, and how they will change even further with exponential and disruptive technologies and automation. In these pages, I will show you what you can do about it, because I firmly believe that we all have the capacity to learn, adapt, and reinvent ourselves.

In fact, this acceleration of change, some of which is brought about by these new exponential and disruptive technologies, is now so rapid that we cannot afford to remain on the sidelines. Unless we truly understand the challenges and opportunities that these bring us, we will suffer from obsolescence—the unfortunate fate of many former leaders and businesses.

This book's main idea is to prepare you to face a world in which *lifetime employment* no longer exists—where the "job for life" scheme is a mere archaeological remnant. This new world requires us to completely and forever banish complacency. We cannot afford to fall asleep in the routine of our lives without thinking about where we are going, where we want to go, and, most importantly, what we have to do to get there.

Through my work with Lee Hecht Harrison, which provides outplacement services and HR consulting to executives and other workers throughout the world, I have spent the past 25 years of my professional career helping people from various income levels and diverse backgrounds look for another job, relocate to another company, start their own business, or enjoy an active and productive retirement. Since 1993, our company's services have helped nearly 12,000 executives to relocate, and we have assisted some 48,000 employees in their job-transition process in Peru. In 1996, we began offering our services in Chile, and I've helped provide outplacement and executive coaching services to more than 1,500 client companies.[1] Worldwide, Lee Hecht Harrison has over 382 offices and helps over 7,800 clients and over 300,000 executives and professionals each year.[2]

Many of the people I've worked with arrived at Lee Hecht Harrison to look for help after leaving their former employers, and most of them were deeply affected by their change in employment status. Many had grown up with the same concepts that my father taught me. The vast majority of these people were well known in their professions, had a top-notch education, and came from reputable companies. Others had even been recognized within their organizations as high-potential employees. Nonetheless, they found themselves on a path fraught with anxiety, desperation, and joblessness—a path that I also crossed years ago. In most cases, their situation had nothing to do with their performance, dedication, interpersonal relationships, or work ethic; other factors had driven their company's decision to terminate their services. Emotionally, their situation was similar to having a marriage dissolve without warning. They watched as their dream of lifetime employment with the same company slipped away.

I've also met many people who weren't very happy with their jobs. They hadn't lost their jobs, but they were actively looking for a new, more satisfying position. Although they enjoyed a certain degree of stability in their current positions, many had fallen into a routine that stifled their personal and professional growth. Using the marriage analogy again, this was akin to staying in a union for convenience or for the sake of keeping up appearances.

Of course, some people do work at the same organization all their lives. Usually, the ones who are still very happy have had the opportunity to grow personally and professionally. For the most part, however, the phrases *all their lives* and *are very happy* are expressions that are increasingly difficult to find together in today's professional world.

With that in mind, this book is not about dismissing the dream of ideal employment and happiness. Although it may sound contradictory, we can get closer to achieving the rewards of an ideal job if we build and strengthen our career potential and work on our competitiveness in order to become more attractive to companies and employers. I approach this topic with a deep understanding that achieving this utopian state is hard.

However, while the majority of the scenarios portrayed in this text refer to people who are executives or who aspire to be executives, the stories I share are applicable to anyone who dreams of finding the perfect job, career, and life. This is especially true now with the ever-accelerating changes in technology and all the challenges that these bring to our personal and professional lives.

I have separated the book into five chapters. Each one can be read independently, but following the chapters in order will lead to a better and more in-depth understanding of the message. This chapter order was determined by three factors, which, in my experience, are vital in our quest to improve our ability to maximize opportunities and find positions that are fully satisfying. These three factors are

- *Clarity.* Clarity will help us understand the new rules in today's employment world and to fully understand the new reality this entails. We examine this in chapters 1, 2, and 3.
- *Good Attitude.* What attitudes are we expected to have in today's professional world? As I discuss in detail in chapter 4, "Maybe you can't do much to change the way you look, but you can change the expression that you wear."
- *Approach.* We need to see and manage our **personal** career as if it were our own (beloved) business! We will look at this in chapter 5.

It's important for you to understand that although I am the author of this book, many of the ideas in these pages are adapted from what I've learned at Lee Hecht Harrison, the undisputed world leader in the outplacement and talent development field. The company currently operates in 71 countries around the world. In Peru, Lee Hecht Harrison handles approximately 85 percent of the executive outplacement services offered locally. Our reputation and our results speak for themselves.

The stories and examples in these pages are my own, based on my personal experiences helping thousands of people since 1993. And as you read the book, you'll find that it doesn't seek to be academic or formal. More than teaching concepts, this book's purpose is to share what I have learned in a friendly, simple, and, I hope, practical manner. I often give this message in person to groups of 500 or more; this book reflects that conversational approach.

The book you have in your hands is an updated and improved version of *Usted S.A.* (*You, Incorporated*), which sold more than 120,000 copies in Peru and eight Latin American countries. *Usted S.A.* has been on Peru's bestseller list since its release in November 2010, second on the bestseller list in 2012 and 2014, and No. 1 in business books in 2013.

I have written this book to help you develop and increase your employability and personal brand. I want to help you improve your attitude toward your work and take control of your career. The ideas in these pages should also help you make positive changes toward improving your personal and long-term competitiveness. Thank you for joining me on this wonderful journey of employability and personal marketing!

CHAPTER 1

THE ONLY CONSTANT IS CHANGE

Not too long ago, this was a very different world. People viewed work not only as a birthright but also as their *private property*. They felt they had the right to a secure career at the company that currently employed them. In some extreme (but real) cases, workers could even *rent* their jobs to others, or, if an employee died, that person's children could inherit the job. Those were the days of an antiquated and rigid system in which an individual, once employed, could rarely be fired, and the vast majority of companies were confined to a small geographical area. To sell products in another country, companies had to set up an additional plant in a new location, but countless restrictions and licensing requirements limited both their ability to trade freely and their freedom to hire or fire.

Today, all of this has changed. Companies are global. They no longer need to open plants in a specific country in order to market their products in that country, and labor relationships are more flexible. A person in a faraway country can do your job at a fraction of what you do it for. They compete with you!

As in any transition, reality changes before the paradigms that sustain it change. Habits and cultural behaviors transform slowly. It may even seem that people turn their backs on change and fail to understand it. What has changed in the world of job relations?

COMPANIES HAVE CHANGED

In the past 20 years, the following words, megatrends, and new ways of working have emerged in the construction of new business realities in the world of work:

Geopolitical and economic uncertainty. Digitalization, big data, analytics. The "gig" economy. Rightsizing. Outsourcing. Mergers and acquisitions. Scale restructuring. New demographic mix. Skills imbalance. Disruptive and exponential technologies. Sharing economy. Crowdsourcing. Automation. Virtual and augmented realities. Artificial intelligence with deep learning. Biohacking. Nanotechnology. 3-D printing. Digital manufacturing. Avatars. Dematerialization and demonetization of technologies. Quantum computing. Machine learning. The Internet of things. Robotics and drones. Chatbots. Renewable energy sources. Synthetic biologies and genomics.

In stark contrast with the past, the following is true in today's world:

1. *Companies are subject to change on an ongoing basis.* Everything in the business and technological environments is constantly changing. Corporate cultures change, and as do their leaders, owners, employees, products, customers, competitors, and the markets they operate in.

2. *Companies carry out dramatic technological innovations.* Organizations that fail to innovate lose their edge, market position, and clients. If they fail to incorporate technology into their business models, they risk disappearing forever.

3. *Companies merge or are acquired by other companies.* In fact, the better a company performs, the higher the probability that it will be acquired by another company. This can happen in a friendly or a hostile way.

4. *Companies are constantly restructured and reorganized to remain competitive and improve efficiency and profits.* A company's success often depends on its ability to reinvent itself. Similarly, our personal success depends on our ability to change, learn rapidly and continuously, and reinvent ourselves.

5. *Rapid market changes, along with disruptive and exponential technologies, force companies*

6. *Knowledge is becoming increasingly valuable.* Education, training, and flexibility to acquire information—or knowing where to find out answers to things we

don't know—is critical to personal, professional, and business success.

7. *The competition is fierce, and it is global.* Everything is now measured by global indicators and international standards. Large companies initiate price wars that affect *all* companies, particularly those that fail to innovate and improve their level of competitiveness.

8. *Companies focus on the core businesses in which they have a competitive advantage.* Nonproductive services or product lines are outsourced or killed off.

9. *Markets and investment companies are placing increased pressure on companies to obtain more and better results in the short- and long-term.*

10. *The digital age is increasingly creating jobs that can be done from any location by freelancers and independent contractors in short-term engagements. That is the essence of a gig economy.*

All of this has affected work and labor relations, and it has overturned existing paradigms and produced new ones. Many people are still struggling to embrace these new paradigms. The labor force and the organizations they work for experience a great deal of change. Organizations constantly redefine employee profiles to ensure that they match the company's current needs. This constantly evolving world is here to stay. Despite the threats of those who push for a return to the past, this trend will undoubtedly continue, and it will be accelerated exponentially by new technologies.

For example, according to the World Economic Forum's 2016 *The Future of Jobs* report, all of these changes could lead to a net loss of as many as 5.1 million jobs globally by 2020.[3] Furthermore, the report highlighted significant changes in job types in this period, projecting growth in computer, mathematics, architecture, and engineering jobs while jobs in office and administrative areas would decline significantly.[4]

"IT'S FOR LIFE" IS NOW "AS LONG AS IT WORKS FOR BOTH OF US"

I always tell the story about my friend's grandparents because it's a good analogy for how we tend to view our relationship with the company we work for. This couple married, had four children, and lived in a city far from the capital. No doubt, they were happy. But unfortunately, one day the grandmother discovered that her husband had had an affair with another woman; in fact, they had two children together. Understandably, the grandmother was heartbroken and furious. She left her husband and took the children with her. Her friends advised against this, saying, "That's what men are like!" But this woman didn't want her husband to be just a provider; she wanted the fairy-tale romance she had signed up for when she first got married. She wanted someone whom she could have a real relationship with, so she stood firm in her decision.

As was the case back in the 1920s, this couple did not challenge social norms, and they continued to keep up with appearances by not divorcing. At the time, divorce was taboo; couples never got divorced, because the institution of marriage was more important than the relationship between husband and wife. The husband, out of *respect* for his wife, never thought of asking for a divorce, because it would've been frowned upon to make the mother of their children a divorcée. In fact, many of the distinguished families of the day refused to invite divorced women into their homes. This couple stayed married for an additional 25 years, but they never spoke to each other again. When my friend's grandmother died, her grandfather was finally free to remarry.

Times have changed. More than likely, no one would accept a scenario like this, because, above all else, people want an authentically loving relationship with their significant other. They want to give and receive love, affection, and passion. Today's relationships are governed by substance, not form.

The same has happened with jobs. People used to see their jobs as lifetime companions, even if the jobs failed to meet their expectations. Companies appreciated loyalty beyond anything else. People who had been fired or had left their jobs were looked down upon and had a hard time finding another job. Things are radically different today. No one has a job because it's their birthright or because they've been there for a lifetime. Companies today do not see jobs that way, and it would be a major mistake for an employee to do so.

A job is now a two-way relationship that will continue only as long as both parties are satisfied. A company will give us a job as long as we add value, contribute to results, generate real achievements, and get along with our colleagues and, particularly, our bosses. Likewise, we'll work with this organization as long as it invests in our development and growth, we find satisfaction in what we do, we get compensated reasonably well, and we feel recognized and valued. *In this context, we will happily work hard and continue to give the company our very best.*

Today, it's clear that we can't assume our relationships with companies will last a lifetime as they did in the old days. As well, most people are no longer interested in keeping up appearances or staying in a situation just because it's convenient, like my friend's grandparents did years ago. The simple fact is this: the majority of us will not be part of a company's staffing plans forever, whether we like it or not!

"UNEMPLOYED" IS NOW "IN TRANSITION"

Years ago, most people assumed that if someone was unemployed, there was something wrong with that person. They might say, "Hmmm, I wonder what he did wrong?" or, "I wonder what happened to her?"

As was the case with divorce, the unemployed were looked down upon and negatively labeled. Today, being in a state of career transition is not at all uncommon. Sometimes you have a job, but other times, you are looking for a new job. There is a lot of discussion about how many times a person will change jobs in a lifetime, and there is a consensus *that the generation of people beginning their careers today will change their jobs at least seven times before retiring, and four of these moves will be involuntary.*[5] In fact, the U.S. Bureau of Labor Statistics found that overall employee tenure had gone down from 4.6 years in January 2014 to 4.2 years in January 2016, and that median tenure among the 25- to 34-year-old group was 2.8 years.[6] In Canada, between 2013 and 2017, the average job tenure across all industries was 103.24 months, that is 8.6 years.[7] In Australia, the average is three years and four months.[8]

Given these statistics, the last thing we should think or say is that someone is *unemployed*, and under no circumstances should we apply the derogatory labels that were common in the past. A person in this situation is *in transition*, whether voluntary or involuntary, and is in the process of finding a new job. Our experience at Lee Hecht Harrison Peru has shown that more than 77 percent of job seekers find a new position that pays the same as their old salary—or more—and in 90 percent of cases, their next position opens better horizons in their careers.[9] This data has been validated by KPMG in Peru.

Most of us will experience job transitions more than once in our lifetime, so we should view these periods as an opportunity to find a new and better job. And since no one is exempt from involuntary transitions, we should take steps now to prepare for this.

JOB SECURITY DECLINES THE HIGHER YOU GO

Given that technology and innovation affect so many different operating processes, many people believe that job security is lower among operators or manual laborers than among those who hold midlevel or executive management positions. This simply isn't true. A plant operator is actually less likely to change companies than an analyst or a manager.

Of the approximately 48,000 people from every job level—manual laborers, workers, technical personnel, professionals, executives, managers, and directors—that Lee Hecht Harrison Peru has helped relocate in the last 25-plus years, almost 12,000 were executives.[10] Among this group, nearly 650 were general managers or CEOs of major companies. Many of them had master's degrees from prestigious universities such as Harvard, Yale, Columbia, the Sorbonne, or the London School of Economics. You might say, "Why do people who have all kinds of key contacts and opportunities, who have studied at renowned universities, or who have held executive positions at very important companies find themselves unemployed at some point?" Well, that's simply how things are today: everything has changed. Even people who have long lists of accomplishments can find themselves out of work at some point. *The truth is, the further up a person goes on the professional ladder of an organization, the less job security that person has.*

Our sample is not necessarily representative of the job market at large, but it does offer an idea of the lack of job stability in today's environment. Even the highest position of CEO, which was once considered immutable, is currently seen as the most vulnerable position in an organization. When the company is not achieving expected results, guess who gets fired? The CEO. In the opposite scenario, if a company is doing well, then it's very possible that another company will buy it. If that happens, the new owners will bring their own people in, including, possibly, a new CEO. Every acquisition or merger affects operations, plants, new businesses, and so forth. That's why direct operating personnel are less likely to lose their jobs than higher-level managers.

The presence of a union may also protect operating personnel in situations that involve redesigning a business. In contrast, executive positions are considered *positions of trust*, which basically means that if you're an executive, then the company cannot guarantee that your job is safe. In many reorganizing scenarios, executives either must leave the company or resign, with no dignity lost.

YOUR SUCCESS IS YOUR HAPPINESS

The meaning of the word "success" **has also undergone a significant change.** People used to associate success with material possessions and everything that these entail. However, it is time to change our perspective. *Success is a reflection of who we are and our level of personal satisfaction with what we do, not what we own.*

A few years ago, I was interviewed on television about success. One of the interviewers said something like this: "Success is primarily defined by having a good job, an excellent salary, or a fabulous car."

I asked him, "Do you consider your mother to be a successful person?"

He said, "Of course!" He seemed somewhat annoyed. (You know how people get when you mention their mother.) Later, he added, "My mother is a superwoman. She has never worked a day in her life, but she's happy and fulfilled. She is a good mother who's very dedicated to her home and family. She has raised five children and is very proud of all of us."

I then said, "You see? Your mother is a successful woman. She is happy with what she does, and that's more important than anything else. And you recognize that she's successful, even if this fails to meet your traditional definition of success."

When we talk about success, we don't fixate on other people's stereotypes of what that means. Instead, we look at how personal satisfaction defines our success.

The quest for success through a job is defined as the search for a career that gives us professional and personal satisfaction while contributing to our development and the fulfillment of our dreams. It's the job that makes us happy on a day-to-day basis. *Success* isn't about what other people want, expect, or need us to be; nor does it depend on what others believe we should earn or what material possessions we should have. *Success* is not what our spouse, parents, or children expect from us; nor is it defined by having the same material possessions as our neighbors, friends, or relatives. *Success must be defined in purely personal terms, and this definition should be based on what each of us wishes to be, do, know, or have in life.* Success should be anchored in the goals we hope to achieve and in our personal or professional aspirations.

YOU NEED TO STAY IN THE GAME

One of my friends married her university sweetheart. They had three children, and, like everyone else, experienced ups and downs in their relationship. As the years went by and the pair settled in to married life, they became complacent and took each other for granted. Neither my friend nor her husband nurtured the relationship, and it was clear they were both unhappy. But, still they stayed together. My friend complained about her husband all day long. According to her, when he came home every day he planted himself in front of the TV, ignored her, and no longer did anything to please her. She wasn't happy.

As time went on, my friend became increasingly bitter. Her other friends and I told her that, if she wanted to give her marriage a chance, she needed to start taking better care of herself. We also suggested that she might try to improve communication with her husband.

She replied, "Why? We are already married and have three kids. Do you really think that anyone else is going to be interested in such a boring guy?"

The day did come, however, when he left my friend overnight for someone else.

Of course, my friend was devastated. Even though she had stopped nurturing the marriage, her husband was a major part of her life. She never thought that her marriage would end and she'd be alone. It took my friend a year to recover emotionally. When she finally felt better, she announced to us, "I'm ready to get back in the game. I want to find someone new who's worth my time and will adore me."

She started slowly and grew more confident as time went by. Every day, she was happier with herself, and eventually she started dating again.

Her ex-husband—who would stop by to see the children and make domestic arrangements with her—started looking at her differently, and one day he decided to ask her out. She made it difficult for him at first, but after a few months of dating, they decided to give their relationship another try.

A year went by, and after the initial romance began to wear off, the couple went back to their old ways of not appreciating each other. Big mistake! They began treating each other poorly again, she stopped prioritizing herself and she put the relationship on the back burner. She assumed, once again, that her relationship was safe, and she became complacent again. The relationship and the marriage ended, this time for good.

My friend had failed to understand that a secure marriage, one that lasts a lifetime, is impossible to achieve without effort and without lovingly nurturing it every day. The same thing often happens at work. When people are looking for a job, they prepare thoroughly, read up on the prospective company, dress well for the interview, are well-informed about company news, treat the interviewer nicely, and work on their network of contacts to ensure they have good references. But once they find a position and have been on the job for a while, old habits begin to kick in: "I have a job, and I'm safe." Then the complaints begin. They no longer value their job, and they make negative comments to coworkers: "My boss is a pain;" "I hate my job;" "I don't get paid enough;" or "They're stifling my growth."

It seems to be human nature that when we feel secure in a given situation, we tend to take it for granted. Yet there will likely be repercussions. A company may not take immediate action to fire someone whose performance is less than acceptable or who has a bad—or even hostile—attitude, because there could be some legal or financial repercussions to carefully consider. However, rest assured that the first chance the company gets, that person is sure to go.

On the other hand, some companies offer castles in the sky to attract talented and hard-working professionals. These castles come tumbling down once the new employee is on the job, and the company fails to meet previous agreements. That approach isn't acceptable either.

It's important to understand that the working world has changed and that both parties have options outside the "monogamous" relationship. Employers who are interested in keeping a good working relationship alive need to nurture it to generate loyalty. And, to feel secure in the employment world, employees need to be truly employable. We must never become complacent and assume, "I've made it!" or "I have a safe job!" because this may not always be the case.

YOU ARE A SERVICE PROVIDER

If we are in transition and are looking for a new job, or if we wish to increase our employability, then we need to learn to successfully identify our accomplishments. This means that we must identify the impact that our work has on a company's results, which includes everything we do to contribute to those results and how we generate value for the company. The achievements and results generated by our work are what help demonstrate the quality we have to offer as employees, or—better said—as service providers. We show that we are effectively doing what they expect of us, what they hired us for, and more.

I see the look on workshop participants' faces when they find out that Lee Hecht Harrison's outplacement program requires them to identify at least 25 accomplishments that they've made throughout the course of their professional lives. "That many?" they ask anxiously. We also ask them to make sure that the achievements they write down are as tangible and concrete as possible.

Many of our clients are afraid that they won't be able to quantify their value or results. They make the mistake of describing what they did and the responsibilities they had, rather than what they've actually achieved—their *contribution* to the results. At the beginning of the process, clients assume that their previous job title is enough to get them back into the job market. When they actually describe their achievements quantitatively, they are fascinated to see the impact of their contributions and are delighted with the achievements and results they have produced during their professional lives. They learn that they really are service providers and that they can offer solutions that create real value for organizations. We will explore the definition of *achievement*, along with quantifiable examples, in chapter 3.

An important point to remember on the road to becoming employable is that we aren't paid just to *go to work*.

....

We are paid to add value, contribute to results, fulfill objectives and specific goals, and satisfy the client's needs.

....

It isn't enough to arrive at the office on time every day. We have to do our work well and go beyond what is expected of us. Obviously, we must clearly understand what is expected of us, how we will be evaluated, and what success indicators are used to assess our performance at any given moment. This means that we must embrace the fact that our relationship with the company has changed. Now, both you and the organization that hired you are service providers. *We need to see ourselves as providers of professional or qualified services.* And this has nothing to do with our position within the company.

For example, we executives like to publicly say that we're executives. But we're also employees, or better yet, under the new paradigm, service providers. This always becomes particularly clear to me when I'm traveling and need to fill out immigration forms or similar official documents that require me to state my occupation. What do I write?

If someone pays us a salary, whether we are the company's general manager or its youngest employee, we're all service providers to the organization that hires us. As you can see, our relationship with our client organization is a two-way street. It's a relationship among equals, as well as a clear, well-defined business relationship. WE are the providers who sell our services to THEM—the organization. THEY hire our services to contribute to their business in order to hopefully generate more wealth and positive results.

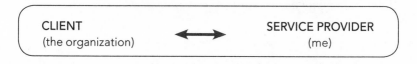

| CLIENT | | SERVICE PROVIDER |
| (the organization) | ←→ | (me) |

 The organization is our client, and we provide it with our professional services.

As an example, I provide Lee Hecht Harrison with my professional services as the company's president. I have a special interest in ensuring that Lee Hecht Harrison is happy with my work as well as my team's performance so that the company continues to renew our contract year after year.

We're fully accountable for our relationship with our client, and it's our responsibility to ensure that Lee Hecht Harrison remains interested in hiring our services, so that we won't be replaced by others who may be less experienced and charge less for their services. We're the only ones responsible for making sure that there's demand for the services we sell. In our case, the company has renewed our contract annually for the past 25-plus years, but there's no guarantee that this will be true in the future.

Whether my team and I are on a company's payroll, charge professional fees for part-time work, or send invoices for our services as freelance providers, the scenario remains the same. What's critical is the relationship between our client (Lee Hecht Harrison) and us (their service provider).

Remember, *we are the only ones responsible for the quality of the services we deliver, and this is the primary factor in determining if we find employment in any other organization.*

EMPLOYABILITY ANCHORS STABILITY

To highlight a key point again, no company can guarantee us a secure job. No organization in the world can genuinely promise that it will keep anyone on the job for life. A company and its leaders cannot even guarantee their own security or continuity. As we have seen, managers are more vulnerable to change than other personnel. The general manager and other high-level executives have less job security than anyone else in the firm.

So, you could ask, "If no company can promise me security, can I do anything to feel safer in the job market?" Clearly, we all need a certain level of financial security to make short- and long-term plans. The greatest change over the past few years has been the change in focus: **Today, the security we yearn for doesn't come from having the same job forever** or even from having a job. **What allows us to feel safe is knowing that we can gain employment whenever and wherever necessary, because we are employable.**

Let's go back to the example of my college friend. She shouldn't have been so sure of her marriage simply because she was *married*; that kind of security can only come from a positive relationship that's nurtured on a daily basis. This couple could've had a good marriage if both of them had made a commitment to remain affectionate and interesting to one another. In the employment world, this means that both parties need to remain *relevant* and *competitive*.

My friend's relationship would've been further strengthened if they had decided to treat each other with dedication and love. Similarly, commitment and respect in the workplace between the employee and the employer help create a sense of harmony and happiness on the job.

As I've suggested, today our security doesn't come from having a job; it stems from the fact that there's ongoing demand for our services in the job market, beginning with the company we currently work for. This continued demand means that if our employer decides that it can no longer keep us on, or if we no longer wish to work there, we can enter the job market knowing that someone else will consider our services valuable. If this is the case, then *unemployment* will only be a short period of transition between jobs or professional activities. There will always be someone who's willing to give us a position within an organization because our services are relevant, competitive, valuable, and will surely lead to growth for the organization.

In addition to achievements and results, it's important for us to have a reputation of being team players who are dependable, serious, and highly professional. This is our best guarantee for maintaining constant demand for our services within an organization.

The security we yearn for doesn't depend on who employs us—it depends on the effort and the positive attitude we put into increasing the constant demand for our services—that is, our employability!

I know that the formula laid out above is difficult to accept. It's more comfortable to assume that security is provided by an outside source and we don't need to make much effort to achieve it. But the security we seek is only achievable if we create it for ourselves, particularly given that many of the old rules no longer apply.

As an example, let's look at the case of the Japanese labor market in the past. Employees at the country's largest companies were "lifers"—they began their careers at a company and stayed there until they could retire with full honors. Changing jobs was rare, and in some cases, it was even considered treason by the employer. Companies rarely fired their employees.

When DBM, a leading worldwide outplacement company, began operations in Japan in 1982, people thought my Japanese colleagues were crazy for trying to introduce the concept of outplacement in Japan, where no one changed companies. Yet today, Lee Hecht Harrison, which bought out DBM in 2011, has thousands of client companies in Japan and locations in nine cities throughout the country. At its enormous offices, our operation in Japan has supported the professional transition of thousands of Japanese executives and employees. What explains all these changes and growth in Japan? Years ago, everyone thought Japan would be the last place to lose lifetime job security, but that went by the wayside even before it occurred in Latin America. In general, average job tenure in Japan is down to approximately twelve years and there are some indications that this downward trend may continue.[11]

It's not that loyalty at work doesn't count or that time of service and work experience are no longer valued. However, these things alone aren't enough to ensure that we'll find or keep a job. As we have discussed, the main reasons we are able to find and maintain a job are related to the results we produce and the contributions we make every day to help an organization reach its objectives. These things, coupled with our professional working relationships, ethics, attitude, and reputation, are the rocks upon which security is built.

··

We are employable when the value we add to our employer is visible, quantifiable, and evident.

··

For further reading see the infographic on page 156

CHAPTER 2

EMPLOYABILITY

Today, employability is the basic paradigm of our working life. Building, developing, and demonstrating our employability is an ongoing task. To do so, it's important to identify our level of employability, recognize its advantages and limitations, and work consistently to improve it.

We have spoken of employability, but we haven't defined it yet. We've seen examples of it, but we have yet to bring together all of its components. This will be useful in understanding its importance. Let's cover these basics now.

WHAT IS EMPLOYABILITY?

Let's consider two of the definitions of employability that we use at Lee Hecht Harrison. Our general definition is as follows:

Employability is the capacity, attitude, and disposition to add value and develop the skills necessary for the tasks at hand and for those that may arise in the future. This also includes the capacity, attitude, and disposition to develop contacts to find or maintain a space for professional contributions—a job, or a client for our services—whenever and wherever necessary.

This means that we must always ask ourselves, "What skills do I need to have or develop to find a job if I suddenly need to do so? What added value must I contribute to keep my job (if I am already employed) or improve my performance?" In sum, we need to ask ourselves what we need to do and know in order to always be considered *relevant, known,* and *valued* in the job market.

Answering and working on these questions will raise the level of our employability, which actually constitutes nothing more than the ability to adapt a set of personal and professional skills to market demands at a specific point in time. The higher the level of our employability, the higher the demand for our services. This is how a range of choices and greater "security" will become available to us.

Here's a more complete definition of employability. Luis Carlos Cabrera, former president of DBM in Brazil, said,

[Employability] is an individual's personal ability to accumulate and maintain skills and to keep her network of contacts and knowledge up to date in order to ensure that she is always in the best position to decide about *her career*.

If we want a more complete definition of employability, we can say that

> Employability is the capability or power that everyone has to maintain or improve their current position, or obtain a new or better position that is at the same or higher professional and personal level at any given time.

....

Quality and *time* are basic elements of employability.

....

Our employability will increase if we can access those jobs and positions that take full advantage of our capabilities (which, consequently, will be higher-paying positions) in the shortest amount of time possible. This will generate the expected accomplishments and results as well as improving our reputation, which will allow us to be in full control of our professional lives. Being highly employable (or having a high degree of employability) allows us to be in control of the decisions we make about our career. So, if we're not satisfied with our job, or we are working at an organization whose values are not aligned with our own, or we are simply unhappy, we have more opportunities to find a better job that can satisfy our needs in the short-term.

EMPLOYABILITY RAISES YOUR OPTIONS

Employability takes place in two scenarios:

1. **Within our place of work.** Employability can come from within our workplace by allowing us to access a higher-value position because we have achieved better results than others. Worst-case scenario, we're employable within our workplace because we are not on the list of people who will be fired and because the company we work for believes that the value we add is more significant than that contributed by others.
2. **Outside our place of work.** If we've decided to go in a new direction or are unable to avoid being placed on the "chopping block," we'll need to put everything that we have achieved in terms of our employability to the test. If we've worked to achieve a high level of employability, we will find a good job—a new space to contribute or sell our professional services to—more quickly.

Most companies these days treat their employees quite differently than their predecessors did. For example, in very competitive industries or service segments, companies *fight* for the best talent, and in some cases they even *steal* the best employees and executives from other companies to improve their results. Wherever there's growth, there is also a need to hire people and retain those who are already working (effectively) at the organization. When there's a crisis, the situation is even more pressing. Most successful businesses have realized that they cannot afford to treat their employees badly in any way, because if and when they do, the most talented employees will leave. And those who usually leave soonest are typically the most employable, because they have better opportunities for quick relocation. These individuals will not put up with any kind of mistreatment. Instead, they will leave in search of better opportunities, more challenges, and more recognition.

At Lee Hecht Harrison, sometimes we're asked why a business invests in our services to help relocate personnel who are asked to leave the company. Our answer? Everyone at a company pays a great deal of attention to the way the organization treats those who leave. Moreover, the best employees are always on the lookout to see if those who leave are treated with respect and are given assistance to relocate. People consider this important because it signals how they will be treated if they happen to find themselves in a similar position in the future. These signals indicate whether a company practices what its leaders preach, including values such as respect and appreciation for employees, and they are concrete proof of how the company reacts when things get complicated and some people inevitably need to leave.

A few years ago, an airline experienced difficulties that illustrate this point. A group of pilots had been complaining about certain working conditions for some time. As a negotiation strategy, the people in charge of employee relations at the company chose not to pay much attention to the pilots' requests. One of the company's executives even went so far as to treat the pilots' representative disrespectfully. This was the straw that broke the camel's back, and many of the airline's pilots and other workers simply resigned. Just imagine an airline that has multiple flights scheduled, but from one day to the next loses a third of its pilots. What happens in this case? Obviously, all hell breaks loose.

When the company's main executives realized what was happening, they tried to convince the pilots to stay by offering them more money and agreeing to their original requests. However, the pilots had already accepted offers from a competing airline, which was more than happy to snatch them up under better conditions.

....

If we were to investigate, we would most certainly find that those who left also had the highest employability levels, and those who stayed had fewer options.

....

This does not happen in all companies or in all business cultures. But more than a few organizations still fail to recognize that their main asset lies in the talent of the people who work there. Some companies have the wrong attitude and tell their employees, "Be thankful, because you're lucky to have a job." These immature organizations won't be able to compete in the long-term, because in today's highly-competitive business climate, where talented people are needed the most, organizations that don't offer the best place to work will be unable to attract or retain the best talent.

If you're working for such a company, it may be that your efforts to assertively and consistently work on your employability will be of little use within the company. However, you can be sure that as long as you work to enhance your employability, you'll have better options outside of that archaic culture. Additionally, your decision to leave may even help the company change how it relates to its employees in the future. In this way, you'll have contributed to making that company a better place while also improving your job possibilities.

Even if the company we work for is less than ideal, there is no excuse for neglecting our employability. Feeling like a victim serves no purpose, and it actually sabotages our growth and development. People with high degrees of employability always have a number of job alternatives. Successful and modern companies compete for their services and, moreover, try their best to retain them. In fact, the more we contribute to a company's value, the more power we have to negotiate in good faith when reviewing our employment status, because they should hate to see us go. But if we create no value, and don't contribute to achieving the expected results—therefore becoming less employable—the company may part with our services at any time.

As we've noted, even if we provide the best service possible and add a great deal of value, we may still find ourselves out of a job. This is because organizations are subject to continuous change: they are acquired, get merged, undergo technology changes, change owners, change policies, change their goals or vision, and so forth. In that case, our employability is taken outside, where we have the opportunity to find a new job or an opportunity to sell our services to a different organization, a job that could be just as good, if not better. This is why *being in transition* is now considered to be a normal and natural state within the professional life cycle. At all times, we need to maintain a positive attitude as well as our reputation as an excellent service provider and driver of results. In this way, we can ensure that our **employability levels consistently remain high.**

Being employable cannot guarantee that we'll definitely keep our current job, but it will make our potential to remain employed much higher than it is for our colleagues who haven't fulfilled this requirement.

HOW TO MEASURE EMPLOYABILITY

There is a popular saying that nothing can be improved or managed if it isn't measured. In other words, there's no way of knowing if we're moving in the right direction and at the right speed if we can't measure it. This is also applicable to our employability: we need to measure it to know where we are and where we're going. We don't need to become experts in mathematics to decipher the formula and mechanisms for measuring something as complex as employability. But we must have some reference points to see if we're constantly improving.

At Lee Hecht Harrison, we have a very simple technique at the office to measure our employability on a daily basis. We call it the *white door* test, because the exit doors at our offices are white. At the end of every workday, as we walk through those doors, we ask ourselves, "What value did I add today? What did I do today to earn my keep?"

For instance, my answers to these questions might include these:

"I spoke with three client companies."
"I closed two contracts with companies that are letting people go to help them relocate the people on their separation list."
"I helped someone find a new job."
"I received a request from a company to send out information regarding a position that they need to fill urgently."
"I prepared someone for an interview."
"I helped develop a personal marketing plan for someone who's committed to increasing her employability."

We need to develop a set of questions to ask ourselves while we're on our way out at the end of each workday. When we can positively answer these questions with a list of what we've accomplished during the day, we can feel safe knowing that we're doing our best to remain employable and marketable.

What happens if we have a hard time pinpointing what we have done to add value, or we feel that we haven't given enough to the company? Say you go through the doors on a Monday and say to yourself, "Hmm, I don't think I did much today, not much at all, but who cares; today is Monday."

On Tuesday, you leave the office and say, "What did I do to contribute today? Actually, I wasn't that focused today. I need to consider that."

On Wednesday, you go through the doors and ask yourself once again, "What have I done to create value for the organization so that they'll want to keep me on, and what have I done to ensure that I'm considered a valuable member of the team so the organization remains interested in renewing my contract?"

If three days go by and you're unable to identify something that you have done that adds value, you're than likely on the road to losing your job, because you are swindling the people who pay you by not contributing. It may sound like an exaggeration, but the need for commitment and an attitude of adding value shows few exceptions.

In many organizations, work contracts are theoretically established for indefinite periods. The organization's executives are constantly evaluating their personnel and their performance. With these evaluations in hand, managers decide who's highly-employable and who isn't in order to develop a list of promotions or determine who might be let go.

In the most advanced organizations, where human resource departments are more formalized, there are many ways of measuring performance, results, potential, and skill sets. These departments rate their employees, or service providers, and later let them know the results of this process. This type of organization also has well-structured systems in place to ensure that people who are seeking promotion and continued professional development can find it within the organization.

Unfortunately, the vast majority of organizations have no such system; even some large institutions have yet to develop a rating system for individuals who aren't at the executive level or who hold key positions regardless of hierarchy. If your organization lacks this system, you need to take the initiative and perform a self-assessment and gather information from others about you. To accomplish this, the first step is to ask your boss or bosses as well as your coworkers how they see you. Your questions should be based on these elements:

- Do they feel that you are competitive?
- How much value do you add?
- What are your strengths and weaknesses?
- How well do you perform against your objectives?
- Are you a team player?
- Do you have the right kind of attitude?

You can also ask your coworkers and internal clients to evaluate you. This information will give you a clear idea of your tangible contributions, and it will help you identify how others view you in the workplace.

Another way to measure employability is to watch and study the job market even if you aren't looking for a job. This way, you can measure the extent to which the market values your position or one similar to what you're currently doing. Just remember: measuring and improving your employability is *your* responsibility, not the organization's.

IT MAY BE UNFAIR, BUT IT'S REALITY

When one of my daughters was younger, she would exclaim, "Mom, that's not fair!!!" whenever something didn't go her way. I would reply that life may not be fair, but that's just the way it is. Similarly, things at work may not always seem fair. For this reason, we need to constantly ask ourselves questions like these:

- What can I do to improve every day?
- How can I grow, develop, and contribute?
- How am I better in my overall performance?

Remember, the *competition* in the market that uses our services is always plentiful, and our competitors may be younger, more energetic, and willing to work for less. As well, our employers may simply decide to try someone new. Returning to the marriage analogy, even when partners do their best to be kind, take care of themselves, pay attention to small details that show their affection, and so forth, one of the partners might still set his or her sights on someone else. That's just life—it isn't fair, but it's reality.

Too many people neglect to stay competitive and build their skills at work. Yet the old excuse for this poor attitude simply doesn't work anymore: "How we do things in this organization doesn't matter, even if it's important in the rest of the world." Believe me—this is no longer the case.

Many organizations, whether local or multinational, use KPIs (key performance indicators) based on international standards. For example, at Lee Hecht Harrison, we need to be as competitive and efficient as any of our colleagues in the 71 countries in which we operate. No one at headquarters will say that it doesn't matter that we're less skilled or talented than those who work at Lee Hecht Harrison in France, Japan, Turkey, or the United Kingdom, just because we're a smaller member of the worldwide network.

Always remember that we'll have a better chance of keeping our position, progressing with our career, or finding a new job or opportunity to sell our services, should we need to do so, if we're highly employable. This is the only thing that keeps our services in demand at any time. Understanding the job market means accepting all of this as truth. Today's rules, whether we agree with them or not, whether we like them or not, and whether we consider them fair or not, are the new rules, and we need to develop a game plan accordingly.

WHAT MAKES US MORE EMPLOYABLE?

Once we understand the concept of employability, its importance, and how to measure it, one question remains: "What makes us more employable?" The rest of this book will be dedicated to answering this question.

The list of topics is long because employability has multiple components. It's a complex issue with many dimensions, including these three elements of employability:

1. Valued Personal Skills (VPS)
2. Demand in the Job Market (DJM)
3. Exposure to Decision-Makers (in the Target Market) (EDM)

....

EMPLOYABILITY = VPS + DJM + EDM

....

Here are the crucial factors associated with each component.

- *Valued Personal Skills (VPS).* We can have many skills, but based on the work we do, they may be valued to a greater or lesser extent by our target market. If these skills aren't considered valuable, our employability will be low. Knowing which of these skills are valued in our field or at our level is essential.
- *Demand in the Job Market (DJM).* Our skill set may be valued by companies, but the job market—which has highs and lows—may be saturated at a given point in time and may not be in need of our skills. In this scenario, the result will also be poor because there's no demand for our services. So, to improve our level of employability, we need to identify what the market

values, determine the market's current situation, and assess the opportunities available.

- *Exposure to Decision-Makers (EDM) in the Target Market.* Even if there's a market for our skills, if the decision-makers don't know we exist, this will reduce our level of employability.

SOFT SKILLS MATTER

Beyond what we know how to do and our technical, managerial, or specialized skills, the market is increasingly interested in our ability to integrate, work as a team, lead, and commit to the organization. Organizations expect us to go beyond what we're asked to do, be assertive, and most importantly, be flexible.

If two candidates have similar backgrounds, experience, and intelligence, then attributes that may seem less tangible can make the difference in who gets the job. This includes values, general attitude, passion, creativity, curiosity, charisma, adaptability, and habits, as well as the capacity to effectively handle diverse social situations (emotional intelligence). Attributes that may seem ancillary will also make a difference, including experience, up-to-date knowledge, interpersonal relations, knowledge of multiple languages, the ability to learn faster, the ability to hack our brains to make them more efficient and productive amidst the challenges of digitalization and automatization, and so on.

We will be more employable if we work on the skills valued by the market, which go beyond our knowledge and intelligence, the university we attended, or the degree we hold. We need to put aside those things over which we have little or no control and instead concentrate on what we can improve. We cannot change our intelligence and, generally, our problem-solving capacity, or our ability to propose brilliant solutions. But we can work on appearing more tactful, less obstinate, and more open, flexible, and adaptable. We cannot pretend that we have a degree from a different university than the one we attended, but we can update our knowledge by frequently attending courses or seminars.

....

To improve our employability, we need to sharpen our work skills and social intelligence skills, while ensuring that others know we're there and available through networking.

....

For further reading see the infographics on pages 157 and 158

CHAPTER 3

IMPROVING YOUR PERSONAL COMPETITIVENESS

As we've covered in the previous chapters, we must be globally competitive, and we can't let our guard down just because we're playing in the local leagues. Today, performance indicators are important regardless of the country in which we work. Technological advances are available worldwide to compare data from many locations objectively and instantly; the information is within everyone's reach, including our competitors. Whether we're an American working in Australia, a German working in Turkey, or someone from Japan working in Chile, the indicators our employers use to measure the quality of our performance are the same. If we assume that working in our home country gives us the luxury of coasting along in our career, then we're making a big mistake that compromises our employability.

It's important to keep up with international standards.

We need to constantly ask ourselves what's changing, what improvements are being made, and what others who are in our field on the other side of the world are learning. These questions are important because these people are our direct competition for jobs.

Improving our employability requires us to work on both our job skills and our social skills. To remain marketable and employable, we need to be both productive and good team players. We not only have to be good at what we do, we also have to give the impression that we're good at what we do. These topics are covered in this chapter, and we will look at two additional components of employability—being in sync with the market and making sure we're visible to those who are looking to hire the services of someone like us—later.

JOB SKILLS

When we are introducing ourselves to the job market, we need to demonstrate not only our intelligence and functional or technical knowledge but also our soft skills and employability. Three points are key to ensuring that we're as competent and competitive in the job market as possible:

1. Recognize the value you add.
2. Stay up to date on the latest trends.
3. Be proficient in various languages and cultures as well as in technology.

A job interviewer will likely ask us about each of these three points. Let's look at each component in more detail.

Recognize the Value You Add

We've already noted that we're not paid to go to work; we are paid to add value. It's important to clearly understand that we're paid to drive achievements, add value, and contribute to bottom-line results. Many people believe that accomplishments serve as *fillers* within a résumé, but this isn't the case. We need to be conscious of what we're doing and how we're contributing to justify our salary. We don't get paid to show up or occupy space, and we're most certainly not getting paid "just because".

Are your achievements and contributions clear to you? In my experience, very few people who are currently employed have a clear and organized list of their achievements accompanied by quantitative proof of the value that they're adding to their job. This requires conducting an ongoing follow-up of our achievements. The first important recommendation is to make a list of our achievements and keep it up to date. This list will be useful when we're putting together our résumé or when we need to provide our boss with evidence of our contributions (for example, during performance evaluations). In addition, the list will come in handy when we're drawing up a career plan or want to ask for a raise or promotion. This list is also going to be very useful in helping us determine if we're actually contributing and adding value as we have set out to do.

How should you create this list of achievements? Before we look at that question, let's define what an achievement is:

An *achievement* is embodied in the things we do that give us satisfaction and allow us to contribute to the organization's goals and strategic vision. *Achievements let us know that we're doing our jobs well.*

For example, let's say that we're in charge of selling something very basic, such as homemade chocolate chip cookies in the north end of a city. We can define ourselves within our résumé as "responsible for selling cookies in the north end." A potential employer, however, is actually going to be concerned only with how many cookies we sold, if we contributed to increasing our company's market share, how many clients we added, how the return on investment on our merchandising efforts may have improved, and anything else that provides concrete evidence that our efforts were successful.

A good way to review our achievements is by using a system known as PAR—Problem, Action, and Result—which is very practical. It involves identifying the *problem* or opportunity that existed at a given point in time, explaining the *action* that was taken, and noting the *results* generated from this action.

Many people say, "But I'm not sure what the results were because I haven't measured them and I wasn't told what they were." This is why it's good to always have an updated list of our achievements. We need to ask what the direct impact of our actions was and what we contributed to the company through our actions. If we keep track of this data, then when the time comes to update our résumé or prepare for an interview with our boss or a third party, we won't need to undertake an archaeological dig to unearth data that dates back years. We will have updated our list of achievements within our résumé, and we will have identified our results using the PAR system—identifying what problems or opportunities arose, explaining what actions we took, and noting the results of those actions.

Above all, we must be aware of the fact that generating achievements and adding value is what we're paid for. So, by keeping close track of our achievements, we do ourselves a big favor by consciously raising our level of employability. This helps to transfer our achievements from the realm of the vague and uncertain, to the concrete and real world of numbers. Every day we need to ask ourselves what we contributed and achieved while defining the value we added to the company through these achievements.

Stay Up to Date on the Latest Trends

Just as we're rarely asked in a job interview to give the equation for compound interest, few potential employers will ask if we have read the most recent book written by a Nobel Prize winner in our specialty. However, there are two areas where we **do** need to stay up to date in order to ensure that our employability stays intact.

The first is staying up to date on national and international news, as well as articles in trade magazines, involving our profession, industry, or the role that we play in the organization for which we work. The second area of interest is technology and everything related to the advances in technology, politics, and business.

How can we keep up to date? Through multimedia, social media, newspapers, books, magazines, specialized blogs, podcasts, webcasts, videos, and apps on a daily and weekly basis. It's difficult to imagine a successful professional who doesn't stay informed. It may sound a bit exaggerated, but professionals shouldn't walk out the door in the morning without first having read, listened to, or watched the news—whether online or offline. During a presentation I gave a few months ago, I placed a great deal of emphasis on this point, and it caused many people to shift uncomfortably in their seats. I received protests such as, "I don't have time to read or listen to the news in the morning," and "I read it when I have a minute or at the end of the day when I get home." Their responses led me to infer that this task was fairly low on their priority list. That's unacceptable. If we're going to be up-to-date professionals, then we can't be taken by surprise by news that we receive in the afternoon at the office or even the next day when it's too late to make a decision that could affect our business.

To shed light on this point, I asked one of the participants, "Did you brush your teeth before coming today?"

"Of course," he answered.

I went on to ask, "And why?"

"Because it's important," he replied.

Everything is a matter of priorities. The same goes for news and information. Anyone who considers themselves relatively educated and informed—and, as such, employable—must read regularly and stay well-informed. Ideally, you should subscribe to various business and trade magazines and journals (and any others of interest to you).

. . . .

It is also very important to be familiar with technology and make it a part of our daily routine.

. . . .

This isn't an issue for millennials or younger generations, but for people over the age of 40, it can still be a sore spot.

Today, for example, we must fine-tune our digital identity and continually update our online profiles. We need to be very proactive in terms of building our image and our personal brand within social networks. Remember that today, more than ever before, people can find out more information about people through Google and LinkedIn—we're tracked whether we like it or not. Rejecting technology or not being up to date with it is akin to professional suicide.

Learn Multiple Languages and Experience Many Cultures

Last year, I worked with a top-notch former financial executive from a US subsidiary. He was about 48, and he spoke only English. After an intense job search, he found some positions, but the fact that he didn't speak any other languages meant that the companies offered him a maximum salary of, let's say, $100,000 a year. Another professional, who had a similar profile and was the same age—but was proficient in Spanish as well as his native English—found positions that offered him up to 30 percent more, and within a shorter time span. In a global market, English, Spanish, and Mandarin dominate all languages. We need to learn at least two of them.

Just browse through LinkedIn job postings, and you will find a number of positions—generally those that are better paying—requiring at least a basic-level proficiency in a second language, whether it's Chinese, Spanish, French, German, Japanese, Arabic, English, or any number of other languages. Globally, a second language is vital, not only because it's advantageous to speak another language, but also because it increases our ability to understand other cultures, and possessing sufficient knowledge of a second language is a definite plus in the employment market. If you're a native English speaker (and chances are you might be if you're reading this book in English), then at least learn Spanish! There are many language-learning apps available that can make this task easier and more pleasant than ever before, at any age. Age is no longer an excuse for not learning new skills or languages—including musical languages and computer programming (which is the language of computers)—to facilitate our connectivity with anyone anywhere in the world.

If you don't know a second language, what are you waiting for? At the executive level, this is like going from the minor to the major leagues. New languages change our lives completely and expand our cultural horizons.

Another valuable attribute in the business world, and therefore important to employability, is related to how much experience and engagement we've had with diversity and other cultures. Contact with other cultures opens our minds so that we can learn more and faster. Cultural diversity is a fundamental value in the modern business world. This experience enhances our ability to share with people who are different from us and contribute with their unique perspectives in any given situation. This allows us to grow as people and as professionals. As we all know, discrimination is unforgivable.

Even traveling as a tourist helps enrich our working lives and expand our paradigms because we're exposed to different cultural realities. But most of all, we have the opportunity to interact with people who think, behave, and live differently than we do. Unfortunately, some people who do have the means to travel more often prefer to remain in the comfort of their own culture. *We need to take advantage of every opportunity we have to expand our horizons both inside and outside our worlds.* No one can take these experiences away from us, and their value far exceeds the money we spend enjoying them.

I know a plant manager who's held the same job for the past 12 years. He hasn't traveled at all during this time, and he hasn't attended any courses, seminars, or lectures.

He hasn't made any new contacts, and he has chosen to live within the four walls of the plant, seeing the same people day in and day out. If this man stops working for his present employer, regardless of the reason, he'll find it very difficult to reinsert himself in the job market, because he's so used to his current world, his "safe place." It will be difficult for him to make new acquaintances at a new job and adapt to a new work environment. How employable do you think this man might be?

SOCIAL SKILLS

A fundamental component of the job search is determining whether or not you fit into a company's culture. This point may be even more important than the preceding ones for the simple reason that no one likes to work with people they consider untrustworthy or whom they personally dislike. Therefore, to be competitive, it's crucial that you demonstrate your ability to implement the following social skills.

- **Maintain integrity (ethics and values).**
- **Manage personal and professional relationships well.**

In addition, of course, you should always have a good and proactive attitude, and show energy and team spirit.

During a job interview, we may be asked about each

of these components. The answers we give to such questions are crucial. Interviewers aren't just choosing an analyst or a marketing director; they are selecting a colleague. If the interviewer will be our future boss, then that person is looking for someone trustworthy whom he or she can delegate to, confide in, and expect to serve as a good representative within other areas of the organization. That's why an interviewer will closely scrutinize a candidate's social skills and emotional intelligence—not just the items listed on his or her résumé.

Maintain Integrity

Not long ago, an acquaintance who is a self-employed professional accused me of being overly *rule-conscious* when I asked him to give me a receipt for his professional fees. He was furious and said that my *business* morals shouldn't apply among *friends*. Thinking about his "elastic" moral code, I asked myself if I would trust his ethics or professionalism. The answer was, "Certainly not!" Can you trust someone who cheats, lies, or *stretches* the truth in any part of their lives and justifies their actions by *separating* one world from another? Aren't you always the same person who lives the same values, despite the circumstances?

Technology is breaking down barriers between our professional, personal, and family lives. Everything is known, everything is discovered, and everything can be instantly uploaded to the web or posted on Facebook, Twitter, LinkedIn, Instagram, YouTube, or in a blog. Can we lie, misrepresent, or cheat scot-free? As time passes, these things become less and less possible. The entire world is watching how we interact in every aspect of our lives, and no one is free from *being found out*. All of our actions are seen, judged, and remembered. Increasingly, there are fewer barriers between the public and our privacy. You are expected to act ethically at all times. The business world does not forgive those who fail to live up to their word or who act unethically, no matter how well concealed. Everything eventually comes out.

None of us wants to risk losing the trust of our loved ones or our employer or clients—now or ever. Obviously, this doesn't mean that we need to act like saints or be paranoid all the time. But it does mean that we need to be transparent and increasingly conscious of the consequences of our behavior. If we make a mistake, we should acknowledge it immediately and take steps to remedy the situation.

We all want to trust people and be trusted by others. This trust—this moral authority—is born out of respecting others, acting correctly, keeping our word, and behaving with integrity.

....

Does it pay to do the right thing and act ethically? It definitely does!

....

This is particularly important if we analyze and plan our personal and professional lives with an integrated short-, medium-, and long-term vision. The ethical mistakes we make follow us throughout our lives. And they'll continue to do so long after we've forgotten about them.

On the other hand, I believe that constantly thinking about what others say about us and pretending to like everyone just to get ahead or get something in return is not the best policy. We all know people who look like they wouldn't hurt a fly: they're so polite and pleasant all the time, even playing the victim with their leaders, bosses, or competitors. But the truth is that they will take their claws out and attack as soon as they get the chance. This isn't a great way to behave either. People like this will eventually get caught up in their own web of deceit.

Doing the right thing, keeping your word, being honest and concerned about others, as well as respecting them, sounds almost boring, outdated. Although these qualities may not seem *exciting*, they make up your character and show your integrity— your ability to make amends for your mistakes and maintain your reputation intact despite setbacks.

If we live by our values, and not by *what everyone will think or say about us*, then we'll become better people and more attractive professionals in the job market. Remember, a good definition of integrity is "doing the right thing even when no one is looking." Our *personal brand* is a reflection of who we are and how we see ourselves.

....

Can we be successful in business and be honest?
Yes. Will this success be sustainable in the long
term? Yes. Can we be a bit unethical, rely on bend-
ing morals, and be successful? Maybe. Will this success stand the test of time? No.

....

Can we play unfairly, scheme, deceive, and work in
businesses that operate with clear conflicts of interest? Yes,
but it won't last. Everything eventually comes to light. Can
we do business and associate with unethical people without
suffering the consequences? No. We are also known by the
company we keep.

I know that many readers may ask, "How can we recognize a decent and ethical professional?" I apply the *no* test.
It's very easy to recognize ethical people when they resist the
temptation to engage in *unethical behavior* even if it costs them
their job, additional earnings, or a business opportunity. Honest people know when to say, "no." And we do it for ourselves,
our careers, our reputation, as well as for our employability
and success. But the main reason we do this is because we have
to live with our conscience and sleep well at night.

Manage Personal and Professional
Relationships Well

Are you good with personal relationships, or are you the
irritating one in the group? Being emotionally intelligent

helps us to successfully manage our interpersonal relationships. This doesn't mean that we should try to get everyone to like us. It means that we should try to understand people and, depending on each situation, show respect, friendliness, teamwork, and collaboration. The boundaries we place on our relationships and how we draw the line between coworkers and friends will be determined by our ethics, values, and interactions with others.

Several years ago, Lee Hecht Harrison was hired by a multinational company that had bought a previously government-owned organization. This company asked us to help them manage the transition process in a compassionate and respectful way, given that it would involve many changes in employees' job descriptions. We weren't involved in the process of choosing who stayed and who left. Instead, the company hired us to help relocate all personnel who were let go. We also provided assistance to ensure that the exit process was handled carefully and respectfully, and that the employees' dignity and self-esteem were intact as they left the company to face the job market.

As soon as we arrived, we were introduced to the executive team. A number of executives had worked at the firm for many years, and they were understandably worried and apprehensive about what was going to happen to them due to the merger. However, there was one executive who looked very calm within the group. He told anyone who would listen that he wasn't worried because he was the only one in the management team with a master's degree from a well-regarded foreign university and, most importantly (according to him), he was the only one in the group who spoke English well. So, he was sure that he would continue to work at the new firm. Unfortunately, he was very arrogant and conceited, with little empathy toward the group: for years, he'd never missed an opportunity to let his colleagues know that he was better than them. Needless to say, because of that attitude, not many people liked him or enjoyed working with him very much.

A few months went by, and the new management evaluated all managers. It was precisely this executive who was the only one on the entire team who was let go from the organization. Why? Because his relationship with others wasn't good; he had made no effort whatsoever to integrate with others. He was arrogant, he was a poor team player, and he had never bothered to develop his emotional intelligence. When this executive found out he'd been let go, he truly couldn't believe it. He said, "I'm the only valuable professional at this company—the other employees don't know what I know—they're a bunch of losers. I made this company what it is today." He clearly wasn't a good team player, and nobody wanted to work with him. It's impossible to work with someone like that.

· ·

Nobody wants to work with arrogant, conflictive, bitter, or resentful people, regardless of their academic credentials or experience.

· ·

Who wants to go to the office to look at the same smug

face, day after day, or put up with the same bad attitude? If we have emotional intelligence, then we'll behave very differently than this executive did. And our career will benefit greatly.

Satisfy the Boss

At the forefront of our employability is our relationship with our boss. We need to understand early on in the game that as long as we work in an organization, our boss will be crucial to our career advancement. We must also understand that we're rarely in a position where we get to choose our boss. The internal system for performance evaluations or organizational climate measurements may allow us to voice our opinions about our boss, but meanwhile, we have to accept that person as he or she is and make the best of it. Therefore, it's important to maintain a productive relationship with our boss even if we don't have the best chemistry or if our work styles are completely different.

Our boss—who represents the company—is the main client for our professional services. As such, we need to meet our boss's needs with the results expected from us, which are key components in our employability. Obviously, we also hope that our boss is interested in ensuring that the relationship flows positively, particularly given that this is a good sign of an effective leader, but his or her satisfaction is our responsibility regardless: our boss is our number-one client, and we must treat this important relationship accordingly.

We need to ensure that our boss is always satisfied with our performance so that he or she will be motivated to renew our "contract" year after year. It's our boss who decides whether we will be promoted, what training we'll receive, whether we're given more responsibilities, and what he or she will say about us when asked for references.

In short, much of our professional future depends on this person, and as such, we need to be attentive to ensure that our relationship with our boss is a productive one. After all, he or she may still be giving references about us for the next 30 years.

 Your responsibility is to ensure that your boss believes you're valuable to the organization.

When my children ask me, "Mom, how much longer do you plan on working at Lee Hecht Harrison?" I answer, "For many years to come, I hope."

When my old boss went to work at another company, I had to travel to Sao Paulo to meet my new regional head. During the trip, I kept thinking to myself, "I need to tell him everything we've done in Peru, including all of our achievements. Lee Hecht Harrison Peru is the best outplacement company in Spanish America, and I need to tell him all about our wonderful team. I hope I can clearly understand what he expects from us and how he wants us to help achieve his vision. I need to know which indicators he'll use to measure our success."

I also said to myself, "I really hope we like each other and have good chemistry. I hope that our expectations for growth are similar, because if these elements don't exist, I may soon be out of his long-term plans." I emphasize *liking one another* because we'll be more employable when, in addition to knowing how to get along with others, we have good *chemistry* with as many coworkers as possible.

Chemistry is even more important when it comes to your boss. Think about these questions: Would you hire someone you really don't like? Would you hire someone who seems to be difficult, arrogant, or unfriendly? Would you hire someone who, although capable, seems irritating? If you could choose, would you be willing to spend hours every day working with someone you can't stand? Definitely not!

. . . .

In the real world, chemistry, emotional intelligence, and interpersonal relationships are becoming increasingly important to our employability.

. . . .

People want to work with other people they like and trust.

Many people are very uneasy with the idea that their boss is their client. Obviously, manager–employee relations can always become complicated by unmet expectations, real or perceived injustices, little or no recognition, or lack of interest in the employee's development. It's also common for people to take unresolved personal baggage to the office, such as problems with authority or adolescent rebellion. Others play victim or confront their boss without considering the consequences of their actions. Unfortunately, these people waste their energy on things that don't make positive contributions to the business or their potential future.

📝 **Remember, no one wants to work with someone they find irritating or who constantly wears a *sour* expression.**

I would like to clarify that I'm not advocating for a subservient or submissive attitude. Quite the opposite. I propose considering that although this relationship, like all adult relationships, is a two-way street, we need to take special interest in ensuring that it flows well and is based on trust and mutual respect. Jack Welch, the well-respected former CEO of General Electric, goes even further by saying, "The subordinate's job is to make his boss shine so that he looks good to his boss. This way, if the boss sees us as a key player in his success story, we will move up the ladder with him."[12]

So, we need to play politics. I am not referring to the negative connotations that are often attributed to politics. *Being political is knowing that you work with people as well as through people and through partnerships.* This involves identifying and understanding the power of networks within your organization, and how they work. Playing politics involves having a clear understanding that your main client is your boss.

Of course, there are situations in which we need to choose to explore other options. If we truly believe that the leader we work for has no ethics or values, isn't admirable, or constantly takes credit for our accomplishments, then we can always try to transfer within the organization. If this isn't possible, then we can always choose to look for another job outside this company. I know that this may not sound practical, but it's a very real possibility. Working side by side with a bad boss condemns you to an unhappy life at work, and if we're not happy with what we do, then it will be very difficult for us to add value to the company. Not only that, but we will bring this cloud of negativity home with us. Putting up with a bad boss is like being caught up in a massive wave that sinks us and condemns us to professional misery. And where does this lead us? Nowhere. There are few things worse that being trapped in a work environment we hate that makes us miserable.

Be Cooperative, Proactive, and Flexible

Some years ago, I was invited to take part in a virtual panel to comment on a presentation made by Jack Welch. Someone asked Mr. Welch what he thought was vital to success in the workplace. His answers, although seemingly very simple, were so valuable that I am sharing them with you here:[13]

- Have a good attitude toward both internal and external clients.
- Work with passion.
- Do more than you are asked to.
- Expand on the topic with your own contributions.
- Take an interest in others.
- Take a deep interest in the topic at hand; don't make it up as you go along.

See how simple it is? If we do all of these things, we *will* be successful at work.

To illustrate Welch's valuable comments, I would like to share a story that I received in an email some time ago. The author is unknown, but the story is in wide circulation on the internet in various forms, where it is usually called "The Parable of the Oranges."[14]

The Parable of the Oranges

Joe had been working at a company for two years. He took his work seriously, was dedicated, and always did what he was asked. He always arrived on time and was proud that he'd never received a warning during his two-year tenure. One day, he approached his boss with this concern: "I have worked very hard at this company for the past two years and I like my job, but I feel that I have been overlooked. See, Fernando was just hired to do a job like mine six months ago and he's already been promoted to supervisor."

"Hmmm," said the manager, "while we're looking at this issue, I would like you to help me solve a problem. I want to give all our employees fruit after lunch today. The corner store sells fruit. Please ask if they have oranges."

Joe went off to do as he was asked. He came back five minutes later.

"Well Joe, what did you find out?" asked the manager.

Joe said, "They sell oranges."

His manager asked, "And how much are they?"

Joe replied, "Oh, I didn't ask that."

The manager then said, "Okay, but did you see if they have enough oranges for the whole staff?"

Joe replied, "I didn't ask about that either, sir."

The manager then asked, "Do they have any other fruit we can get instead of oranges?"

Joe said, "I am not sure, sir, but I think..."

The manager then asked Joe to sit down for a moment.

The manager picked up the phone and called Fernando. When Fernando arrived, he was given the same instructions that Joe had received.

Ten minutes later, Fernando was back, and the manager asked him, "Okay Fernando, what did you find out?"

Fernando said, "Sir, they have enough oranges for the entire staff and, if you prefer, they also have bananas, papayas, melons, and mangos. Oranges cost $1.50 a pound; bananas run $2.20, mangos are ninety cents per pound, and papaya and melon each cost $2.80 per pound. I was told that if we buy in bulk, we can get an 8 percent discount. I have asked them to set aside the oranges, but if you choose another fruit, I need to go back to confirm the order."

The manager then said, "Thank you, Fernando, but excuse me for a second."

The manager looked at Joe, who was standing there with his mouth open.

"Joe, you were saying?"
Joe uttered, "Nothing, sir. That's all. Thank you."

What a great story, don't you think? You have no idea how many times I have sent this story via email to an employee rather than reprimanding him or her in person for not showing initiative.

....

Proactivity, collaboration, service, and doing more than you're asked to do when possible—all of these things will definitely improve your competitiveness and employability.

....

If we can top off all of these attributes with flexibility and adaptability, we will be well-equipped and always a step ahead of the competition.

"Change alone is unchanging," said Heraclitus. The worst thing for our career and our employability is rigidity and fear of change. This attitude, which is the opposite of the attributes I've just listed, is accompanied by reactivity, lack of cooperation, and tunnel vision. These are all the opposite side of the same coin, where inflexibility and fear of change are engraved on one side and flexibility and embracing change as a positive thing are engraved on the other.

People who blindly defend their comfort zone—fighting to protect the status quo and their sense of safety—are overwhelmed by any change within the company. They refuse to accept the new reality, and they say no to everything, assuming that their power is being threatened. This type of person is not very employable.

Companies need people in their ranks who are capable of seeing opportunities within changing scenarios instead of only threats.

Why are people so resistant to change? No one wants to HAVE to change their routine or how they think or act. No one likes the uncertainty that comes with change, and even less so if it means that his or her status, role, or identity may suffer.

For example, at Lee Hecht Harrison, whenever we are helping two companies that are preparing to merge, we sit down with executives from both parties. It's immediately evident who will go through conflict within the new organization. These people either consciously or unconsciously sabotage everything associated with the merger. They become defensive when asked about their team's performance or their own, they tend to put down others, and they become angry or uncomfortable if their coworkers fraternize with employees from the other company. They promote conflict, sometimes unconsciously and without real ill intent. Many times these people are unaware that their attitude is sabotaging not only the process to integrate the teams but, more importantly, their own future.

APPEAR COMPETENT

Some people believe that being concerned with image, appearance, or body language is superficial and inauthentic. In the world of yesterday, today, and always, as long as human beings are led by their senses, trust their instincts, and are guided by what they see, hear, smell, and feel, having a positive image will continue to be a critical factor when it comes to interpersonal relationships. At the very least, taking care of our appearance will keep us in the game. For some, this will represent a competitive advantage over those who believe that concentrating on one's external image is trivial and superficial. Looking good helps raise our self-esteem. People can't just *be* competent; they have to *appear* competent. This is discussed in more detail in chapter 5.

There are four important ways to ensure that you always seem competent.

1. Show that you're trustworthy and keep your word.
2. Act with consistency and integrity.
3. Communicate your ideas well.
4. Radiate energy, enthusiasm, positivity, and good vibes.

Let's look at each of these essential actions in more detail.

Keep Your Word

"Yes," said the manager of a large company. "Of course I remember that I gave my word. How can I not remember?

I also know that I promised to pay for these services, but I never signed anything. So how do you expect me to explain to my boss that I have authorized this payment if I have nothing to back it up with? You know how it goes; everything has to be signed in blood."

Can you imagine how you would feel after hearing this from the manager of a large company that used your services? *I have previously emphasized that I believe our word is just as valuable, if not more, than any written document.* There's no excuse for not honoring our word, ever—in doing so we fail others as well as ourselves. Executives' words are their company's word, and failing to keep promises has repercussions on their honor and image—as well as their company's.

The manager then went on to say, "Do you honestly trust everything your clients say? Do they really keep their word? What world are you living in? I guess you work with serious and socially responsible companies. That makes it easy. We, on the other hand, have to cut expenses where we can, and we are often forced to do away with formalities. Honoring commitments and social responsibility are for fat cats."

Does this sound surreal? No doubt! Is this really commonplace? Thankfully, no.

All over the world, among serious businesspeople, we're expected to respect the agreements we've made, even if they haven't been written down. Serious companies and people believe that our word is enough to trust us completely and do business with us. Standing our moral ground is worth as much if not more than any possible financial gain. This is the foundation of the integrity and congruency of the line workers, technicians, office workers, entrepreneurs, executives, and leaders whom we all put our trust in.

....

Our word, just like our ethics, values, and reputation, constitutes the foundation of our real and moral success as professionals with true vision and a modicum of self-esteem. It's also a core driver of our employability, business continuity, and, of course, personal success in business.

....

The *easy* way of doing business, which favors cashing in personal favors to get ahead, is a thing of the past. It has no place in a serious business environment. We all have likely heard horror stories or have witnessed shady business dealings, but we should not turn a blind eye to these practices. We need to let people who act inappropriately know that we will no longer do business with them, much less trust them.

Maybe you're asking yourself how the story of the manager ended. This man's boss, the general manager, found out about this employee's unethical conduct from various suppliers. He personally called all the parties to apologize and subsequently honored all commitments. I can only imagine the talking-to this executive got from his general manager after that.

The question is—did this executive learn his lesson?

Will he be trusted in the future? The answer on our end is no, never again.

Be Consistent

Another related positive trait is consistency, because the opposite—the unexpected—creates stress. Ideally, we should always be consistent in our actions, as this trait makes us predictable, in the best possible way. Consistency allows people to read us and predict our actions. In this way, people will understand us better, feel safer when they interact with us, and put more trust in our work and opinions.

Who hasn't had that awful boss or colleague who smiled and backed us up one day when we made a mistake only to make a fuss over the same thing the next? If the people who work with us cannot predict our attitudes and reactions with some degree of certainty—and, on the contrary, consider us to be unpredictable—then we'll have a significant issue with our image and communication with them. Our bosses and coworkers won't know how to treat us or what to expect from us on a day-to-day basis if we're unpredictable.

To be more employable, it's important to develop an organized, disciplined, and responsible demeanor. No one can trust or work comfortably with people who are inconsistent and create awkward situations wherever they go.

Communicate Well

Today, few things are as important as communicating well both orally and in writing through email, presentations, social networks, and so on. If we communicate well, in an organized and concise manner, we prove our intelligence, education, and interest in our audience, because we're making the effort to be understood.

Speaking and writing well about what we have read and learned is important, and there are techniques that can help us quickly improve our communication skills. This is why it's always a good idea to enroll in public-speaking courses that can help us deliver effective presentations. Why should we speak in public? Speaking in public ranges from one-on-one conversations to addressing a small group of potential investors for our start-up, or even presenting before a hundred or a thousand clients. It allows us to influence others, negotiate, and convince friends, our boss, or even the board of directors of our point of view. Good public-speaking skills help us make a significant impact on how a situation develops. Moreover, it helps us to properly communicate an idea and influence others.

It's become increasingly important to fine-tune our communication skills—this requires perseverance, practice, and technique. I used to be petrified of speaking in public, but I pushed myself to learn techniques to handle public speaking effectively. I believe these skills have contributed greatly to my employability. In fact, I now enjoy speaking in public. I experienced something similar when I began to write articles for magazines and newspapers. I now write regularly for some publications, and I've published 800 articles and videos with more than six million visitors. Of course, I'm also the author of this book (and you can decide for yourself whether I've done a good job or not).

Radiate Energy, Enthusiasm, and Passion

Imagine that I want to work at your company and you are interviewing me. Picture me seated before you with my head down. In a barely audible voice, I say, "I want a job. It isn't that I like the position, but I have no other choice, because I need to take care of my children. Help me. I don't want to do anything that requires too much effort, because my back hurts if I work too much. But give me a job, please, because I need one." Would you hire me?

Unfortunately, many people still believe that they will get a job simply because they need one. The truth is, we're hired to do a good job and add value to the company. And what differentiates one applicant from another is showing how much we want the position and proving we're truly passionate about becoming part of the company. So we must consider the *passion factor* in the equation.

However, one of the traits—or rather, shortcomings—that many of us suffer from is fear or discomfort of showing "too much" energy, desire, and passion. Perhaps we believe that by appearing overly interested, we will seem desperate. Instead of showing excitement, we often put up walls, appearing disinterested. But it's important to realize that nothing sells better than enthusiasm. Our drive and passion have to come through in our eyes. We need to say, "I want to work here because I like what you do. I have researched the company, and I really like its values, products, and way of doing business." We need to speak energetically, instead of keeping our distance by saying, "It seems interesting, and I think I could get used to working here."

Sometimes we forget that by showing emotion and enthusiasm, we become more *attractive* professionally. The sparkle in our eyes is an expression of personal interest—it demonstrates our authentic desire to be part of something. And this makes all the difference.

Continue to Learn

....

Continuous improvement is a habit that we must adopt to improve our employability.

....

Some people say, "If the company doesn't pay for my training, I'm not going." Some time ago, I was working to relocate a client. When I asked him to describe his weaknesses, he said that he knew little about computers.

"Well, that's a real problem!" I said.

Next, I asked him how this was possible, since I knew that his former employer had provided training for its staff.

"They offered us a lot of courses," he said. "But I never went because they were always held at inconvenient times.

Imagine, on top of all the work I put in, they thought I should use my free time to take these courses. And they didn't pay overtime for this! I didn't want to take computer courses just for THEIR benefit."

"What a quandary," I said. "But now that you're looking for a job and you know nothing about computers, whose problem is it? Yours or the company's?"

"Gosh," he said, visibly concerned. "I hadn't really thought about it that way. So the training would've been for my benefit. Just look at everything I let fall through the cracks! I never worried about improving myself that much, and I never expected that I would need to find another job. I thought that after working at the company for so many years, I was going to retire there."

It is also a mistake to believe that older employees are not capable of learning new things or don't have the desire to do so. At Lee Hecht Harrison, we have worked with clients over the age of 60 who have learned about programming, marketing, finance, and a number of other subjects. This has helped them jump-start their careers, and it has improved their personal lives. In fact, by acquiring new knowledge, they've opened doors that may have otherwise stayed shut. Training and learning open up a world of possibilities, allowing us to connect with people with different perspectives. This can give us a new perspective—a different dimension of humanity—and it ensures that we remain relevant and competitive.

Age doesn't limit your ability to learn. Many believe the adage that "you can't teach an old dog new tricks," but it simply isn't true. Learning has nothing to do with your age or college degrees. In fact, it's a matter of willpower, desire, discipline, and attitude.

Constantly look for relevant courses and seminars to take. Not all of these courses need to be expensive. There are thousands of options, and many can be taken online or through apps for free. At Lee Hecht Harrison, when we see a résumé that indicates a client graduated in 2008 but hasn't studied anything since, we ask her, "What did you learn afterward? What else have you studied? Nothing?" If that is the case, then we become concerned about her employability and chances for a successful relocation.

If we lack training and haven't acquired new skills, then we're not as relevant as we should be in today's job market. Training in different areas gives us a broader perspective of the world, which will influence the way we handle any problem and opportunity that may come up in life or on the job. *By constantly seeking further education, we increase our level of employability.* We need to take advantage of any available time and resources to better ourselves. If such resources are not available, then we must try to find them. Our employability is well worth the effort!

A story attributed to Albert Einstein recounts how a woman asked him, "How can I make my son more intelligent?"

Einstein replied, "Read him fairy tales."

The woman must have doubted the impact of reading fiction, because she persisted.

"And if I wanted him to be much smarter?"

Einstein replied, "Read him more fairy tales."

Imagination and creativity arise whenever we expose ourselves to and practice the things that imagination and creativity have produced: the arts, music, literature, and science. Remember, Einstein was a violinist.

For further reading see the infographic on page 159

CHAPTER 4

YOU, INCORPORATED

As we have explored in this book, the majority of us, if not all of us, sell our professional services. As such, we are essentially a service company. It doesn't matter how we're paid for these services: whether we're on a payroll or offer professional receipts or invoices. In all cases, we need to manage our careers like an efficient business. If this is the case, what's our business called?

(Write the name of your own company here)

Let me use my case to explain this concept in more detail. My company is called Inés Temple, Incorporated. This entity cashes the paychecks I receive. Some people believe that a businessperson is someone who owns a stand, a bakery, a startup, a service company, a consulting firm, a telephone company, and so forth. However, if we work for a third party selling our services, then we are also businesspeople. We need to look at our careers as our most important enterprise.

....

Our most important business is our career. Our career is our business!

....

I'm not saying that if you wish to have another business you should refrain from doing so. By all means, go for it. But remember that in any scenario, you will provide your enterprise with your services as general manager, assistant, operator, cashier, or possibly even all of these at once. You need to clearly understand that your primary business, which usually gives you your livelihood (and in turns lets you pay the rent), is the one that sells your professional services.

I recommend that you register your company's name and URL online. It isn't that expensive, and it gives you the opportunity to establish your name, your personal brand. Mine is *www.inestemple.com*. So, what's yours? Think about it, listen to how it sounds, write it down, and dream about it. This is your company's name. Congratulations! You now have a clearly identified brand for your professional career!

YOUR NAME IS YOUR BRAND

We need to take care of our personal brand. We should protect its reputation and ensure that people recognize it and know what it stands for. We want people to tell others that we're great at what we do. On the contrary, we don't want anyone saying we're lazy, unreliable, dishonest, inept, or bad. We all know how much time and effort goes into building a good reputation, a good image, a good name, and above all else, clearly showing what our word is worth. *Your personal reputation can open doors and generate credibility and trust. It's the basis for employability as well as long-lasting, socially responsible businesses, and personal relationships at every level.*

A good reputation is always earned. There are no short-cuts to a good reputation, and the process of building it requires honesty and sacrifice. Your good name will endure over time if it's based on integrity, ethics, and values, which underpin all aspects of life.

Building and protecting our reputation doesn't mean that we'll never fail or that we'll act like saints all the time. But if we make a mistake, or have done so in the past, it's important to make amends with humility, authenticity, and a real determination to learn from it. Hard work, bulletproof honesty, respect for our word, and integrity in every one of our actions are the only ways to build a pristine reputation.

No one likes to hear that they don't have a good reputation. It's a good idea to ask others from time to time where we stand with them and find out whether we're living up to the image we think we own. It's always easier to accuse others of jealousy or selfishness rather than owing up to our responsibility in building and protecting our reputation. Of course, we can't expect everyone to like us and appreciate us as much as we think we deserve. But the responsibility for building and protecting our reputation is ours and ours alone.

Let's look at an example. At Lee Hecht Harrison, we were working with an executive in his outplacement process. He had passed the initial tests of the company of his dreams with flying colors, and he had moved on to the final stage of the interview process. But as life would have it, the CEO of the company that was about to hire this candidate mentioned our candidate's name to his own tennis partner. The tennis partner said, "Don't hire the guy. He's a sore loser. I've played tennis with him. He throws a fit when he loses, and he insults everyone, including the ball boy."

"That's strange," said the CEO. "I met him in suit and tie, and he was a real gentleman."

"Sure," said the CEO's friend. "But just watch him with a racquet in hand."

When our candidate found out why he hadn't been selected, he said, "But what does one thing have to do with the other?"

Of course, these points are related because, as mentioned in the discussion of consistency and trustworthiness, we have to be the same person at all times. Whether we're in a suit and tie or wearing tennis shoes, our personal brand and our reputation follow us wherever we go, 24/7.

I once met a top executive who made a lot of money and was very high-ranking. However, his references told us, "He's nothing but smoke and mirrors. He sells himself well, but when the rubber hits the road, he won't even open an Excel spreadsheet." We had a difficult time placing him in a new company because he had earned the reputation of being lazy.

Speaking of personal integrity, I also know of another well-known, respected man who appears in all the newspapers. He acts like he's holier-than-though, shows up in plenty of pictures with his family, and appears unblemished in the public eye. However, his behavior behind the cameras is reprehensible. He leads a double life and does little to hide it, not even out of respect for those involved. As someone once said, "If you cheat on your family, how do we know that you won't cheat the company?"

. . . .

Our name is our brand for life, and it's in our best interest to protect it.

. . . .

WHAT DOES "YOUR CAREER IS YOUR BUSINESS" MEAN?

Your Career is Your Business means that our personal brand is on display every single day. We represent our brand and the person who sells the professional services of this brand—in other words, ourselves. Accordingly, we have to protect our brand by acting and living with integrity and professionalism at all times: we need to do everything we can to protect how others perceive us. This is of utmost importance, particularly if we move in different circles throughout our daily lives.

Some people believe that we only need to behave

properly in our professional world, and that in our personal lives we are entitled to be disrespectful or dishonest if we want to. This isn't true. As we've discussed, *we must be the same person at all times, regardless of where we are at any given time.*

When you are truly committed to the essence of your personal brand, you're aware of the fact that it follows you wherever you go. You know that you alone are always responsible for protecting your brand. This may sound exhausting, but it's true.

Think of a professional ballet dancer. You may ask, "What do professional ballet dancers have to do with employability and managing a personal brand?" Well, they repeatedly use the following expression: "Always on stage." In other words, they behave as if they are always in the spotlight—always standing up straight and always being crystal clear about the role they're playing on and off stage.

WHAT ARE WE SELLING, AND WHAT ARE THEY BUYING?

Basically, we sell our services, which are a set of skills, interests, and values, which we could theoretically apply on the job. Our skills are everything that we can do. In fact, our achievements, abilities, talents, knowledge, and results are outcomes of our skills. Everything we want and like to do and all the things that motivate us, in turn, make up our interests. And our values are our ethics and our work style. All these factors combine to create the perfect scenario from which to contribute. As the owners of our company, we need to think about how we want to manage it, and we need to identify our goals and responsibilities within the enterprise as well as the position(s) we will hold within our company. Here's a list of some of the positions that we might hold in our company/career:

- CEO
- CFO
- Head of Research and Development
- Head of Marketing
- Head of Sales

YOU ARE THE CEO OF YOUR OWN CAREER

What is the CEO's primary role? He or she must design a long-term vision, set the course, create strategies and policies, and be the face of the company, concerned with its visibility and perception among other things. I love one of Seneca's sayings: "If one does not know to which port one is sailing, no wind is favorable." In other words, if you have no goals in life, you can be sure you'll be going nowhere fast.

Years ago, I heard about a study that made an impression on me. They wanted to find out which factors had an impact on people's future success. They set out to discover if ethnic or gender differences, place of origin, religion, social, or cultural factors had anything to do with success in life as defined by each individual. They interviewed 25,000 young people who were finishing school and asked them to fill out a long, in-depth questionnaire. Twenty-five years later, the survey participants were all between 42 and 43 years old. The researchers followed up with them to see how successful they'd been and ask them what they attributed their success (or lack thereof) to. The study found that 3 percent of the sample felt that they had been tremendously successful in all aspects of their lives—more than they had ever dreamed. Another 10 percent said that they felt they had been successful in meeting their goals both personally and professionally, and they were also satisfied with their financial situation. The majority—70 percent—claimed that they were satisfied with how their lives had turned out. The remainder of the group—the final 17 percent—indicated that their lives had been a failure, and they were unhappy with the course their lives had taken. Often, these individuals needed welfare assistance in order to survive, had poor family relationships, neglected their health, and, in general, felt they'd been dealt a bad hand in life.

So the researchers asked themselves these questions: What really determined which individuals would succeed and which would fail? Was this due to just one factor or to a set of multiple factors? Were the factors demographic? Was success due to "luck" in life?

After a thorough analysis of the data, the researchers found that at age 18, the 17 percent who later said that they felt like a failure had answered the question "What do you want to do with your life?" with a vague or negative response, such as, "I don't know. Don't ask me;" "I haven't really thought about it;" "I have no idea;" or "I don't want to think about it right now." Similarly, when asked "Do you want to study, or what do you want to be when you grow up?" they had responded with "I don't know;" "I have no idea;" "I'll figure it out later." These young men and women hadn't planned for the future. At 18, they had asked nothing from life, and they had formed no plan for "later." Then, years later, this was exactly, in their opinion, what they had gotten from life: nothing.

The people who were part of the satisfied 70 percent were the same individuals who at the age of 18 had responded to the question "What do you want to do with your life?" by saying they had goals, such as having a good job, raising a family, buying a home, owning a nice car, traveling abroad, and sending their kids to good schools. They wanted to become part of that large middle class who lives comfortably. And that is precisely what they achieved.

The individuals in the 10 percent—those who declared they were very satisfied with their lives all around (not just economically) —had said at the age of 18 that they already knew exactly what they wanted to do with their lives. Some of these people hadn't followed their initial plans to a T, but they still had formed plans, goals, and objectives, and they had recognized that they would have to work hard to achieve them. These individuals had identified dreams and ambitions—and they had dared to go after them.

The final 3 percent, who felt they were extremely

successful and had achieved more than they had ever planned for, had formed clear goals, ambitions, big dreams, and well thought-out objectives at 18, which they had actually written down. As you may have noticed, writing down their goals, plans, and objectives was the defining factor in their success. Furthermore, they periodically reviewed these goals and objectives to evaluate their progress and change course as needed. Since they had set the goals down in writing, they were able to measure and manage them to bring them about.

The differences in degrees of success among the different groups in the study correlated with the level of ambition of the goals that the young people had established for themselves and what they had actually done to accomplish these goals.

The only problem with this fabulous study —quoted in numerous books and articles by business people, business coaches, and self-help professionals— is that when we searched for the exact references for this book, we discovered that the study had never been carried out![15] The mentions I had come across over the years were that the study had been conducted in Yale or Harvard, but it turns out that neither of these universities had conducted the study, nor any other university for that matter. Well, until recently that is.

Dr. Gail Matthews, a professor from Dominican University of California, did carry out a study to see what effects writing down one's goals had on one's success.[16] She also added a commitment factor to the four-week study. Dr. Matthews divided her recruits, whose ages ranged from 23 to 72, into five groups to test different factors on the outcome. Group 1 had to think about the goals they wanted to accomplish, rate them in accordance with a number of characteristics (such as difficulty, importance, feasibility, and so on), but not write them down. Groups 2-5 had to type in their goals on an online survey and rate them as well; Group 3 was asked to add action commitments; Group 4 was asked to add action commitments and send these to a friend; and Group 5 was asked to send these along with a progress report to a friend every week.

The results clearly showed that those who wrote down their goals, Groups 2-5, all performed better than Group 1, who had simply thought about their goals. Those who sent their commitments to a friend, Group 4, performed better than those who didn't, and those who added a weekly report to a friend, Group 5, performed much better than the rest. Overall, those who wrote down their goals and shared them with friends had a 76 percent success rate, while the group that only thought about their goals had a 43 percent success rate.[17]

The interesting thing is that each group had more or less accomplished what they set out to do, regardless of the age of the people involved. Bottom line, they achieved the goals they had envisioned for themselves, no matter how few or how many.

In our search for the references of the Harvard/Yale study, we also came across a Forbes article explaining why it is essential to write goals down if we want to achieve them. Mark Murphy, the author of the article,[18] explained that writing things down helps us remember things on two levels, by providing visual clues (when we write them down on paper and put them somewhere that we will see them) and by "encoding" them in a part of our brain that helps us to recall the things that are important to us. He also explained that people who wrote down their goals in great detail – including pictorial cues– had 1.2 to 1.4 times greater chance of accomplishing those goals.

In short, there is plenty of evidence pointing to the importance of writing our goals down in order to fulfill them!

Note: Don't ever get discouraged if you are no longer 18. During the past 25 years, I've worked with many people who are redesigning and finally taking control of their careers, and I've seen time and time again that it is never too late to write down your goals, work hard, and achieve them. I've seen countless people over the age of 40, 50, and even 60 successfully change the course of their careers and lives once they sat down to write the business plan for their most important business: their own careers.

Would you build a home without a blueprint? Would you go to an empty piece of land, shovel in hand, and begin to dig just like that? What do you think would happen when one of your workers asked, "Hey, where should we make the kitchen?" Would you dare to respond, "I don't know; maybe we should put it back there in that corner"? You'd be crazy to do that. You can't start building without a clear idea of what you want, how you want it, how much it's going to cost you, and whether or not you can afford it.

DEFINE YOUR CAREER PATH

We need to clearly define where we're going in our professional lives and we need to have intimate knowledge of the specialty that we wish to pursue. For instance, if you're an accountant, then you need to know which skills the people who are hiring accounting experts look for. The same goes for organizational psychologists (or any other job). If you have studied psychology and want to pursue a career in this field, then you must know what's involved. After this initial investigation, you should clearly define what you want to do with your professional life, how much time and effort you're willing to put in, what you're willing to sacrifice, what you need to learn, and where you can go to fill that knowledge gap.

In his book *The 7 Habits of Highly Effective People*, Stephen Covey says that the best way to set long-term goals is to plan in reverse, which means we should start with the end in mind, namely the day of our death.[19]

Let's do something extreme, as Covey suggests. What do we want the day of our death to be like?

Our first reaction may be, "That sounds crazy!" But just imagine for a moment what we want this day to be like. I'll go first.

With all the advances in health technology, rejuvenation, and longevity, they say we will be able to lead healthy lives until we're well over 100. I'm going to be a little bit provocative here. I want to live until I'm 108 years old. I would like to get to this age with all my faculties (mental and physical). I want to be surrounded by loved ones, to feel loved, and to be content. I'm already working on this goal: I stopped smoking, I eat well, I exercise five times a week, and I get regular physical checkups. I don't want to die poor, but I also don't yearn to have a huge mausoleum, either. I think I'd be just fine having a good coffin and, God willing, I'd like to be buried in a nice cashmere dress.

I'd like to be remembered as one of those old ladies with white or purple hair who's elegant, fun, interesting, and above all, deeply loved, even respected. I would like my life partner to be there grieving over the loss of the love of his life—he'd better do this, or I will haunt him nightly! Obviously, I want my three children to be there. I imagine they'll be very sad that I'm no longer around. My grandchildren and great-grandchildren will also be present and grieving. In my mind, this will be the purest manifestation of the love and affection that united us in life as a result of a very close and healthy family relationship. I believe that my family is the most important thing in my life.

I don't want to be that cranky old lady who "finally kicked the bucket." I don't want my family to be lying in wait for the will to be read because I was too busy working to spend any time with them—I definitely don't want that! And, finally, I hope a lot of people will go to my funeral. This isn't about ego or vanity. I just want to see a true expression of the positive effect of my work on people's lives and their quest for employability. I would like to think that some of the people whom I've interacted with will remember me because my work had a positive impact on them. I'd also like to believe that I was able to contribute something useful to their lives. So if this book, my articles, videos, posts, or blog are of use to any of you, you are cordially invited to my wake. (That's a joke!)

Each of us will envision the last day of our lives in a different way. Some may say that they want to see their nation's flag draped over their coffin, while others will say they have no interest in how it plays out. But one thing is certain: this exercise will help you define your priorities and nudge you to do something about it. You'll also have more insight about what you need to do to make sure that your last day on Earth will go as imagined.

MAKE A LIFE PLAN

Another important point to consider when defining our career path is the need to make a life plan. If you can, take 30 minutes today to think about the following questions:

- What do I want to do?
- Where do I want to go?
- What do I want to do with my company, my professional life, or with the business I want to start?
- What do I want to do with my personal life, health, and family?

During these 30 minutes, with timer in hand, think about these questions. Also take 30 minutes every quarter to answer a follow-up question: *How much progress have I made?* Isn't this what companies do? Don't they put together a business plan every year? Don't they review the results every three months? Don't they compare their initial yearly budget with actual sales and costs? Aren't they evaluated according to these indicators within their organization? Remember, our company or career is our primary concern because it belongs to us and pays the rent. We have to evaluate ourselves objectively because if we don't, how can we determine whether we are personally successful or not?

IDENTIFY YOUR DREAM

The first thing I ask people who come to my office looking for help in finding a job is, "What do you really want to do?" Most people look at me perplexed; few can clearly state what they want. However, in order to help them, I need to know what their work objectives are.

Jokingly, I ask them to imagine for a moment that I am their fairy godmother who can grant them all of their wishes. I also ask them, "What would you love to do or be? What makes you vibrate or shine? What is your dream job?"

Most of them are smiling by this time, and almost all of them tell me their job dreams. However, strangely enough, very few people seriously think about making them come true.

I think that many people feel that dreaming is something that belongs in the world of fantasy and that their dreams are divorced from what is truly possible. They don't see their dreams as the seeds of attainable goals or objectives—real and tangible.

I'm sad to say that many people don't even dare to aspire to achieve their dreams, and most people do not link their dreams with what they want to do with their working lives. And I say *sad*, because my 25 years of experience has shown me that if you don't know what you want, you'll never get it.

So, my work begins by helping people to visualize and design that future job or dream organization. (Although I'm talking about the world of work, this tool is equally useful for your personal life.) I help people to project, define, create, invent, and dream their next activity—to look into their future and to aim to realize what they saw. I help them to clearly define what they want to achieve.

For many, this is a very new adventure that is hard for them to embark on, but I insist that they carry through on it. It is vital that they be able to recognize, value, and put to use the human capacity that we all have to imagine and create our own futures. Similarly, I invite you to write down your clear goals and ambitious, measurable, and quantifiable aims... and get to work! Continuing your career begins with good foundations: the objective.

Nothing makes me happier than hearing the stories and then seeing the results obtained by those who dared to dream and who achieved not only their goals and work objectives, but even their most ambitious business dreams. Lee Hecht Harrison Peru keeps statistics on it, and the results are so tangible that we report them annually. These success stories are inspiring and moving, and they confirm that we can build our reality by working clearly to achieve our dreams.

Talking about making dreams come true in the business world always comes with risks. To the most skeptical, this idea can sound flimsy or fanciful. However, I'm not worried about those skeptical looks, because the many positive work and personal experiences in the area back me up.

I know that dreams can become the starting point to achieving great goals. Sharing this idea, letting others know that their dreams can inspire and direct them, is my main incentive. I firmly believe that we design our future. The exercise of defining what we want, need, or wish for and making a plan to achieve these things, brings us closer to fulfilling those dreams, goals, or objectives. It puts our subconscious to work, aligns our actions, lends coherence to our daily actions, and puts the universe to work in our favor.

GO FOR THE MEDAL

The guest speaker at the DBM annual convention that I attended some years ago used to train the U.S. Olympic fencing team. He shared what he had learned during this time from the athletes, who are highly talented and, of course, incredibly competitive. He explained that during a pre-Olympic qualifying competition, four people reached the finals. One of the athletes had dreamed of being an Olympian all his life. He had envisioned entering the opening ceremony bearing his country's flag. He had always wanted to wear his country's colors and hear his national anthem playing in the background as he walked before the cheering crowd. He was a great athlete, dedicated, and hard working. He had always wanted to be an Olympian, and his dream had come true.

Another finalist had decided very early in life that he wanted to be an Olympic medalist and stand on the medal podium. Like all great athletes, he trained day and night. This young man won the bronze.

The next finalist had reached the Olympics with a deep-seated belief that he would stand on the winners' podium, and he was committed to doing everything necessary to take home the gold. He won the silver medal.

And the last of the finalists went to the Olympics with only one thing on his mind: he had learned all the secrets of his sport, he had practiced relentlessly, and he had no doubt that he was there for the sole purpose of taking home the gold. And he did.

All of the finalists may have had the same talent and athletic abilities; they were all world-class athletes. They had the same discipline, dedication, and passion. The difference lies in the goals they set prior to the competition, because in the end, *we achieve what we set out to do from the beginning—whatever it is that you have dared to dream.*

For the business that is our career—remember, our career is our first and most important business—we must also decide where we want to go. We should determine what we want to do with our personal services, career, and professional lives. Where do you want You, Incorporated to go this year? How are you going to position your company and your brand?

Let me share with you four additional helpful questions that I heard in a seminar some time ago.

- What do I need to continue doing?
- What must I stop doing?
- What do I need to start doing?
- What do I need to avoid?

As you can see, answering and developing these questions will provide you with a winning path to your goals.

HARNESS THE POWER OF AMBITION

I really enjoy working with ambitious people. They know what they want, have clear goals, and push themselves to achieve them. They accept challenges and enjoy them: they know that these challenges are necessary to advance and learn.

Ambitious people take their destiny into their hands and don't sit there waiting for someone else to hand it to them on a platter. They have willpower and determination. They know where they're going and what they've got to do to get there. They are able to transform and create themselves according to their dreams and ambitions, always watching for the opportunities that exist for those who are willing to see them and strive for them.

Ambition is a great motivator to grow and develop. No one is successful without ambition. Those who aspire to be more, know more, do more, give more, or have more possess a purpose and a powerful internal engine that drives them to dare to dream bigger and to go further. Ambition moves them to go forward and achieve what they propose. When ambition is well channeled and applied with values, it is a reflection of a healthy self-esteem and a greater capacity for abstraction and visualization of the future. Ambitious people shine when they approach their goals. They vibrate for them, and they have a contagious enthusiasm to reach them. They inspire and motivate others.

It is important to emphasize that being ambitious does not implicitly mean that you do not have any values or ethics. Nor is it synonymous with a lack of control or manipulation, as is often thought. Some people do not value ambition. They fear and distrust it (almost as much as they fear the success of others). People easily confuse it with excessive ambition, as if every ambitious person was capable of harming others. Of course, there are many people with unlimited ambitions— stereotyped as the villain of telenovelas—who are capable of anything to achieve their goals. But just because these kinds of people exist doesn't disqualify those who have a healthy and positive level of ambition.

Conversely, as the study we discussed earlier revealed, people without ambition ask little of life, and that is what they get: little or nothing. They have no dreams, vision, direction, or destiny, and therefore, they rarely get any-where. Some are conformists while others are passive and lack motivation. Many are bitter, without understanding that their lack of ambition is what sabotages their future: they aren't able to imagine it, and therefore, they cannot create it for themselves. People without ambition tend not to be loyal to themselves. They don't have the courage to risk success, and they don't bet on themselves. Unfortunately, it's as if their wings had been tied and they didn't realize it.

It is up to us to teach our children the power of ambition and big dreams. They are the important engines of personal and collective success. And that ambition can—and should—be for the benefit of others and the common good.

This also extends to politics. We should always demand a very clear vision of our country from those who will shape our future—with ambitious and challenging goals that inspire us all to achieve them. Only then will we achieve the prosperous, fair, and equitable country that we want and deserve!

IDENTIFY MATCHES FOR YOUR SERVICES

If we understand today's working environment, we know that there are different places where we could sell our services.

1. To the nation, as a public servant or a member of the military or police force.
2. To private corporations, which may be large multinational or small startups, local companies that are small or large, publicly traded companies, or family businesses, as an on-staff employee.
3. To nongovernmental organizations (NGOs), which are usually nonprofit organizations, also known as the third or voluntary sector, as an on-staff employee.
4. To individual clients, as a self-employed contractor who offers consulting services, offers professional services, or manages a franchise.

It's important to investigate all of these options to understand how our personal objectives could fit with each of these areas.

YOU AS YOUR CFO

This position, CFO of (insert your name) Incorporated, allows you to buy your professional freedom. What does this mean? **To be truly employable, we need to be free.**

What does it mean to be free in the job market? **It means having at least six months of savings to cover our fixed expenses.** These funds should be earmarked solely for this purpose. That way, the day we feel trapped in a dead-end job, get assigned to a bad boss, or are absolutely miserable at work, we can quit and look for another job without worrying about how we're going to pay for electricity, water, and telephone bills, or more importantly, our kids' expenses.

This isn't easy. I know there are a thousand other things that we need to save for. But I can assure you that there is nothing worse than being a prisoner at a job that makes us miserable. Personal satisfaction is the pillar upon which our professional lives are built. And as I learned years ago, our wealth is measured by what we save, not what we make.

Ideally, we should start saving when we are young to make sure we have the freedom of movement that money affords. However, it's never too late to start. Don't get stuck in a situation where you don't have the freedom to quit because you won't be able to pay your bills.

YOU AS YOUR HEAD OF RESEARCH

We sell our professional services. To do this, we need to know the quality of the services we offer, and we should continually evaluate them to make improvements and remain competitive. An important part of our job at Lee Hecht Harrison involves working with clients to identify their abilities, skills, achievements, and results. Why is this important? Because it helps us understand our motivations, goals, and values. We also need to see if we're truly competitive in today's market and identify those skills that require improvement. Through this process, we determine our strengths and weaknesses. You need to do the same.

BE LOYAL TO YOU

Our career success and satisfaction are anchored in a simple concept: being loyal to ourselves. What does this mean? It means that on the professional level, we should like what we do and have talent for it. Let me give you an example where that isn't always the case. Have you ever seen the television show *American Idol*? When some participants sing atrociously but think they're wonderful, they often act shocked, depressed, or angry when the judges tell them the truth. I often wonder if these people have ever listened to themselves before competing. Obviously, no one in their right mind would aspire to a career as a singer if they were tone deaf and had a terrible voice. But on the flipside, we also shouldn't pursue a career that we don't like just because we have a talent for it, either. I am not proposing that we change professions when we have reached a certain point in our lives—a drastic change like that can be very costly. But we can think about what we really want to do and what we can do well. *Being loyal to oneself is the foundation of professional happiness.*

To be clear, being loyal to ourselves doesn't imply being disloyal to the organization that has hired our services. On the contrary, if we do something we like and for which we have talent, we will achieve objectives with greater ease and be content in the process. This will be reflected in our efficiency and productivity.

I had a very interesting and brilliant Australian professor when I studied at New York University. He used to say that he couldn't believe that he enjoyed something so much and that he was being paid for it! When I heard this, I said to myself, "I want to feel like that someday."

. . . .

There is nothing better than enjoying our work. This generates a virtuous circle where we become more involved because we love what we do, and, as a result, we do it better. This virtuous circle produces the desired results of satisfaction and career success.

. . . .

YOU AS YOUR RESEARCH AND DEVELOPMENT MANAGER

The Research and Development (R&D) manager at You, Incorporated needs to know your strengths, abilities, weaknesses, talents, faults, achievements, motivations, and goals to ensure that you can consistently present a new and improved version of yourself every day. In other words, we need to continually reinvent ourselves because otherwise the competition will pass us by. Let me show you a table:

Table 1

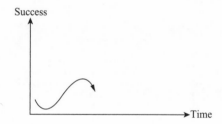

This is the typical growth curve of a company, business, brand, career, or product. At the beginning, we incur pre-operating expenses to get our company, business, brand, or career off the ground. Next, if things go well, an important stage of growth will follow. After this, we will hit the maturity stage, and next, a natural decline will inevitably start.

This curve mirrors the law of life. In years past, when a company or brand stopped growing, it was relaunched. This used to be known as re-engineering, restructuring, or reorganization, all of which were meant to give the company a second wind by repositioning itself. For example, when a detergent brand began to show a decline in sales, it was relaunched with green stain-fighting crystals to ensure whiter laundry, or repackaged with 20 percent more product for the same price. Professionals, when things weren't going their way, might have enrolled in a master's program or a course to relaunch their careers. But those old rules no longer apply. Today, the growth stage—the path to success where we do our best—is also the most dangerous. Why? For one simple reason: the so-called "success trap."

Table 2

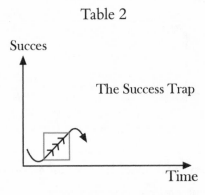

Companies go through the same phases as people in their careers. Just when we're certain we're doing well, when we think we have the magic formula and the master key in hand, we tend to say, "I'm here and I've made it—this is the formula for success. So why should I change or improve if I am doing so well?" You've heard what they say: "If it isn't broke, don't fix it."

....

Do you know what the main problem is within the stage of success? Arrogance.

....

Technically, people and companies that feel they've already "made it" stop making any effort to grow, change, learn, and improve. They also lose interest in further training, coming up with new alternatives, generating new ways of doing business—in short, innovating. Consequently, they fall behind. *Complacency and arrogance are employability's worst enemies.*

The only way to continue being successful is to make changes from a place of strength—in other words, while we're still growing. If we wait to fall on hard times to shift gears and build a new version of ourselves, it might be too late. Just compare the growth and time curves in the following charts. The chances of being successful if we make changes during the growth phase are higher than those if we wait to change until we're in decline.

Table 3

OPPORTUNITIES FOR SUCCESS WHEN THE
TIMING'S RIGHT

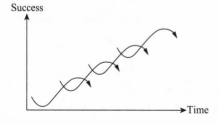

Table 4

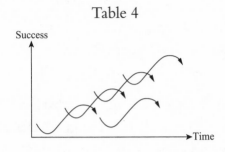

....

> To be employable, we need to continually seek to change and improve, particularly when we're doing well in our careers.

....

YOU AS YOUR MARKETING MANAGER

As our career/company's marketing manager, we must be intimately familiar with the benefits connected with our brand. Why are the benefits we offer superior to those that the competition offers? I often play a joke on participants at my seminars and conferences. First, I ask them to turn their heads 45 degrees to the right. Once all heads turn I say, "You're looking at the competition. Now look to the other side...Once again, you're looking at the competition."

And so the point here is this:

- How will we outperform the competition?
- Which product(s) will we offer?
- What type of packaging do we need?

- What's a fair price to charge?
- Who's our target market?
- How should we advertise or promote our services?
- How are we going to distribute our product?

We also need to play fair—no foul play allowed! If we're businesspeople selling our services, then it isn't enough to be good; we must also be perceived as such. We need to identify our competitive advantages and measure our technical knowledge to determine what we know vis-à-vis others:

- Where do we stand out in terms of our professional skills?
- What interests us?
- What are our points of differentiation?
- How are we different from or better than others?

We need to know all of these things. But be careful: this is not an exercise in patting ourselves on the back; it is solely meant to help us identify the strengths of the services we offer. That way we can figure out how others see us.

As children, we are all taught that it isn't enough to be good; we need to be perceived as such. *When marketing our professional services, we need to remember that perception is reality.*

People will treat us as they see us. If they see us as successful, enthusiastic, and energetic people who take pride in what we do, then they will treat us accordingly and value what we offer. If we look tired or morally bankrupt, or if we speak negatively about ourselves, we'll be treated as such. When we speak well of ourselves, people only believe about 50 percent of what we say. But when we speak badly about ourselves, people believe 100 percent of what we say. Many people, without realizing it, have the wrong internal conversation with themselves, which translates to external damage to their personal brand.

OTHERS KNOW WHO WE ARE

During a coaching session with me, the general manager of a very important company in the mining sector said the following words on two separate occasions, "I may not be too smart, but I work very hard."

I asked him, "Why do you keep saying that?"

He was a brilliant man, but he had grown up thinking that he wasn't smart. The worst thing was that I had already heard this same comment about him from someone else: "He isn't the brightest bulb in the box, but he's a very hard worker."

The market had already bought into what he said about himself.

Beware what you say about yourself. And as soon as you catch yourself saying something negative, stop yourself immediately. As we've discussed, it's very important to not only be capable, but to seem like you are. We need to have presence, attitude, dignity, and a sparkle in our eyes. We will see this in more detail in the personal marketing portion of this book.

Machiavelli once said, "Everyone sees what you appear to

be; few experience what you really are." Just as being employable requires us to be good from the inside out, in personal marketing, we must focus on projecting our attributes outward.

BUILD AND PROMOTE A SOLID REPUTATION

Imagine that you're an attorney and the owner of a law firm. How do you find clients? Do you chase the police or criminals? Do you put up public signs? Obviously not! If you're a doctor and own a private practice, how do you find patients? Do you spread illness in order to bring in clients? Do you put up billboards saying, "Excellent doctor! 298 successful gallbladder operations with only 2 deaths on the operating table?" Of course not!

So how do lawyers and physicians find clients and patients? They do it through recommendations and references from contacts and previous clients. What do positive relationships do for us? People recommend our services, even without our asking. Would people recommend us if we offered subpar services?

Imagine that you're the best doctor in the world and you decide to sit in your office, hands folded on top of your desk, waiting for patients to knock on your door. Are patients going to arrive? What's missing here? Besides being good at what we do, knowledgeable, and having documented achievements and results, what else do we need? We need contacts and relationships, because these people own our reputation. Their opinions of us will determine what they say about us, and therefore, what others think about us. What should these contacts and patients say about us? They should say that we're good at what we do and that we provide high-quality services.

All of this is a package deal. If we're not good at what we do, we then won't have a good image. But if we're good, serious, and professional, but no one knows it and therefore can't share it, what does this do for our employability? Not a thing.

Imagine that you go to your family doctor, and he or she says, "Your gallbladder isn't working, and we need to take it out."

"Who's the best surgeon?" you ask. "Please recommend the best person for the job."

"Well, you can go to see my colleague Dr. Green or another colleague, Dr. Wilson," says your doctor. "Both of them are good. Visit them, listen to what they have to say, and choose whichever one seems right for you."

So you go on exploratory visits. You meet with them and choose the surgeon who makes you feel more comfortable and leaves you with the impression that he or she knows more or is more experienced. Maybe a friend tells you that Green is a good doctor based on an operation he performed on her brother a while back.

Now that you have two favorable recommendations for Dr. Green, three days later you are lying in a hospital bed, wearing surgical scrubs, and a cap. You are unconscious, you are surrounded by people who are practically strangers, and one of those strangers is wielding a surgeon's knife. Just a few days ago, you didn't know him. So why do you trust this doctor, and why is your life now in his hands? Because your family doctor and a friend told you that he was good, and because during your visit with him, he made a good impression on you. He then operates on you and removes your gallbladder.

Do you see? This is how it works. *It's called the power of word of mouth.*

In order to figure out how others see us, we need to ask ourselves the following questions:

1. Are we doing our job well?
2. What do people think of us? How do others see us? What do they say about us? How do they perceive us?
3. Are our colleagues, former colleagues, former bosses, neighborhood and school friends, and in general, the people who know us, aware of what we're doing? Are they aware of all the good things we've done?

If the answer to that last question is no, then how will we find clients for our services? How will we find someone to recommend us?

Perception can do a lot for us. Consider these questions: What reputation do we have in the market? Are we known for being lazy or hard working? Do we have a reputation for being intelligent or a bit slow? Are we empathetic? Do most people like us or are we the kind of person that everyone hopes will cut their visit short? Are we seen as proactive and positive, or are we perceived as negative and indecisive? Do we give off bad vibes? Are we one of those people who radiate positive energy, or do we create conflict wherever we go? Do others see us as being strong or as constantly needing help? Are we smartly dressed people who represent our organization impeccably or are we the ones who need to be hidden from view when clients arrive?

Do we smile often? Do people consider it a pleasure to be with us, or are we bitter and constantly complaining that life isn't fair, the boss isn't fair, that things never go well, and on and on? Are we considered sociable and friendly? How do people see us? What are we really like? Are we pleasant people that others will enjoy spending time with if their flight is delayed at the airport? Can we hold an interesting conversation for a few hours or do people hide behind a book when we strike up a conversation? Are we cultured and well educated? Is it pleasant to do business with us? How do others perceive us? Do they see us as people with whom they'd like to work? Are we people whom others would like to have as bosses or employees? In sum, do others see us as people who they'd recommend?

Personal marketing begins with our image, which begins with what we think of ourselves. How do we see ourselves? How do we want people to see us? As a well-rounded person? Or as sloppy and disorganized? What do we want?

The image you project is what you think of yourself. Our tone of voice is fundamental, as is our body language, if we want to consistently highlight our best features. We should speak positively about ourselves and our personal growth. Nothing sells better than someone who is enthusiastic about his or her opportunities. If you are asked, "How are you?" then you can answer, "I'm happy. Things are going well, and I am sure they'll go even better in the future." You need to look good, smile, walk energetically, be enthusiastic, and show your passion for learning and growing. No one wants to associate, work with, or have anything to do with negative, vengeful, or aggressive people.

We all crave acceptance and approval, but we must give these things to ourselves first. *We also need to come across as passionate about what we do and enthusiastic about the future.* This reminds me of something that a friend once told me, "Enthusiasm literally means *possessed by a god, inspired.*" That certainly rings true to me.

YOU AS YOUR HEAD OF SALES

Who are the salespeople for our services? It's estimated that nine out of 10 people who are currently employed in an organization found their last position through contacts, relationships, or references. This is not the same as using our influence to secure a position. I say this because using our influences as leverage or having a friend find us a job simply because we need one are no longer valid methods for finding employment. In fact, both went the way of the typewriter some time ago.

Who owns our reputation? Our contacts.

Our reputation may begin with us, but it's anchored in

our contacts and the connections we have with others. We need to know how to properly manage our contacts and connections.

....

As we discussed earlier, our network of contacts, which we can call our network of trust, must be developed and constantly updated.

....

Sometimes, when people are successful, they stop working on their network of contacts because they feel it's no longer necessary. Conversely, when people feel like they're failing, they tend to feel less comfortable tapping into their network because they're emotionally at a low point. However, we can't just work on our network of contacts when we need it. In fact, life will become quite complicated if we begin to make a contact list just when we are between jobs. Instead, we should constantly cultivate our network of trust. Then our contacts will speak well of us, not only because we do a good job, but also because we have developed a good relationship with everyone inside our circle of trust. This is something that we need to manage proactively throughout our lifetime, at every turn.

For further reading see the infographic on page 160

CHAPTER 5

PERSONAL MARKETING

Let's summarize what we have learned so far. All jobs are temporary: no job is forever, unless we die in the office (and nobody wants that!). All jobs are like seminars: we need to pay a great deal of attention, learn, and generate results. All jobs are an adventure: we never know what's going to happen next. We also need to seek complete satisfaction through the job we have rather than wishing for something that may or may not change, such as a raise, a new boss, or the ability to take on new responsibilities. If we're not satisfied with what we're doing right now, we will never be happy. We also have to watch our attitude with our internal and external clients and remember that our main internal client is our boss, who represents the organization. We need to learn how to develop a positive relationship with our boss. We also should keep in mind that our equals, coworkers, and supervisors, as well as direct reports, are also our clients. Our external clients not only are our customers; they also are great contacts and connections to have and nurture.

We should also be passionate about our work, do more than what we're asked to do, expand our circle of influence through our contributions, be truly interested in others, avoid lack of preparation at all costs and, of course, find ways to improve ourselves every day. Our attitude is absolutely vital to our success. Our enthusiasm, our drive to work hard and meet our objectives, and our commitment to always being involved determine just how employable we are.

We have already spoken about the success trap, and that the worst enemies of an employable and successful professional are arrogance and complacency. This is why it's so important to use a simple and direct approach with our network of contacts. It's a challenge to talk about our achievements, abilities, and talents with humility and without arrogance. This is one of the things I want to transmit to you.

MAKE A GOOD IMPRESSION

We no longer have the luxury of **not** doing personal marketing. In today's world, we need not just to do it; we need also to do it well. I read an article about an interesting study conducted a few years back. The researchers wanted to analyze nonverbal aspects of teaching and effective evaluations of teachers. How did they test this? They filmed professors teaching a class and afterwards took out three 10-second silent clippings of these classes. They showed these clippings to students and students were asked to rate the professors on a scale of one to nine on 15 different aspects of the teacher: accepting, active, attentive, competent, confident, dominant, empathetic, enthusiastic, honest, likable, (not) anxious, optimistic, professional, supportive, and warm. The students filled out the surveys, which were collected and filed.

The same professors then taught these students for an entire semester. When the semester was over, the students completed the same evaluation. Incredibly, when the researchers compared both evaluations, the answers were impressively close, even after a whole semester. Furthermore, the study was repeated showing students shorter clips, and surprisingly, the before and after results continued to be close. The study concluded that people generally do not deviate from their first impressions, and that these impressions are quite effective judgments.[20] *Every day, we generate first impressions, and not just with new people.*

When I arrive home tired after a long day at the office and see my children, I can tell their state of mind and mood with just one glance. With each day that passes, people become more intuitive. Interviewers who are higher up on an organization's ladder tend to become more subjective in the interview process. A high-ranking executive can take just one look at a candidate and *know* if he or she will be a good fit with the team, if the candidate is what the organization needs, and if that person has that special twinkle in his or her eyes. Fair or not, it is what it is.

Of course, there are ways to mitigate the risk of choosing the wrong candidate with interviews and questionnaires. But in the end, when candidates reach the final round, the person who's chosen from the group of three finalists with similar profiles is picked based on chemistry. **By chemistry I don't mean which candidate seems nicest. I'm talking about the fact that we interviewers choose the applicant whom we feel in our gut will do the best job and with whom we *click* with best. This person must also fit into the organization's culture. In the end, this is nothing more than guesswork, and the decision is entirely subjective and intuitive.**

Interviewers consider, "Can we spend 10 or 12 hours a day with the person we're going to hire? Can we picture ourselves interacting with him or her day in and day out?"

. . . .

When we introduce ourselves, people form an opinion of us based not only on what we say or our tone of voice, but also on the signals that we send through our body language. This is why we need to focus on energy, enthusiasm, strength, passion, and drive.

. . . .

The Reality of Human Communications	
Words	7%
Tone	38%
Nonverbal language	55%
Total	100%

Source: My own based on the information obtained from Simon Holliday's "Spread the word: what Mehrabian really tells us about communication."[21]

To understand personal marketing, we must begin with our image. What others see is what we're trying to communicate. What we try to communicate is what we think of ourselves. We have to ask ourselves, "What am I trying to communicate?" When we dress up for an interview, we want others to know that we are serious, responsible, committed, capable, and maybe even elegant. This reflects how we may be seeing ourselves.

We need to take a closer look and ask ourselves, "Do others like what they see, or do we need to change our style?" When we see people who are sloppy, what does their appearance tell us? I am not promoting stereotyping; I don't think that everyone should dress and act the same. However, it's important to recognize that each environment has its own set of rules for personal appearance. We need to determine the rules of each place beforehand so that we can make a proper impression.

Clearly, how others see us is important. Consequently, although we can't live to please others, we should try to put ourselves in other people's shoes to understand how they see us, what we transmit, and how we present ourselves. This will help us stay relevant, and it will improve our level of employability. It's our responsibility to not only be employable, but also appear employable, and make sure that others see us as that way. This will elevate our perceived value in the market.

For instance, it is important to take a second look at the photo you've chosen for LinkedIn and make sure that it transmits the image that you want to convey to whomever you intend it to reach. We have done extensive research regarding how potential employers look into what you post in your different social media platforms. We must remember that we are the same person in our social and professional lives; there is no longer a division between the two. At the same time, we must be coherent in what we project across all social media platforms. Nothing is private anymore. In fact, our research shows that some 60 percent of those who lost job opportunities did so because potential recruiters did not like the images projected by the candidates.[22]

PRACTICE "POSITIVE COMPLICITY"

Let's look at the concept of "positive complicity." We should treat everyone the same, and with respect, regardless of their job title or ours. This means striving to connect with their human side rather than becoming entangled in power struggles. Whether we're the president of a company or a night guard, we should treat others with respect, and conversely, we should expect to be treated with respect, equal-to-equal. Being the CEO or the night guard doesn't mean we can't address each other as equals because we think we have to "know our place." I've seen plenty of people who're intimidated by people in high positions—they start sucking up to that person because they're not seeing this person's human side and are instead fixated on his or her position within the hierarchy. This prevents them from establishing a sincere relationship. The other person immediately senses that the special treatment is granted just because of the position rather than because of who he or she really is as a person.

The opposite is unacceptable—ignoring people or being rude and disrespectful to them because you consider them to be *beneath* you. This isn't just a matter of bad manners; it shows that we have yet to evolve as humans in terms of social intelligence. We need to address people as equals, human-to-human, and always respectfully. This is the only way to establish relationships that will grow into friendships, which will allow us to expand our circle of trust more quickly.

....

Remember, people like us because of how we make them feel.

....

CREATE YOUR HALO OF SUCCESS

We create our own halo of success. Have you ever eaten at a restaurant that's always empty? Surely you prefer not to. If it's always empty, it must be for a reason.

Sometimes we give other people the impression that we're like an empty restaurant. This happens when we constantly say bad things about ourselves to anyone who will listen, such as, "I'm not doing well," "I'm unlucky," "People are mean," "Life is tough," "I didn't get the promotion," "I don't get paid enough," or "They don't treat me well." Such statements tell the whole world, "Come and eat at my restaurant. I am begging you to be nice because no one has come in for the last three days. The fish is rotting inside the fridge, the fruit has dried up, and the waiters aren't earning any tips. Do me a favor and please come by."

Many people send this message unconsciously and are convinced that people will eat at their restaurant, even if it's only out of pity. In fact, the opposite is true. We all want to go to successful places that are full of customers, a clear sign that they are good. By creating a halo of success, we make a positive impact on other people's lives and show the enthusiasm and passion we put into everything we do.

Success breeds success. How do we transmit success? Through energy and enthusiasm. Enthusiasm is the energy that fuels and creates the future. Let's look at it in a different way. Some people say, "How can I show that I am successful if things aren't going well right now and I'm not at all happy?" This is where enthusiasm comes into play. Although things may not be going our way at the moment, enthusiasm leads us to have faith in what's to come because we believe things will undoubtedly improve in the future. In this way, we shore up our confidence, excitement, and passion about achieving our goals, and we transmit this conviction to others.

We need to convey positivity and passion. Years back, many people had the habit of *playing the victim* and would say things like, "Oh no, poor me; everything goes wrong in my life." Many people were also afraid of appearing too successful for fear of attracting bad luck. We shouldn't necessarily *show off*, but we should certainly impart our positive attitude. In other words, we should let others get to know us, without arrogance, and set the example that we can really achieve what we set out to do in life. This is inspiring.

Leaders need to have the courage to overcome barriers and fears to inspire and energize others. We need to show energy as we speak and walk through life. If we drag our feet, feel sorry for ourselves, or yawn every few minutes, then we're not generating a halo of success, injecting others with our energy, or inspiring anyone.

The quality that probably best defines people of value is their desire to learn. This desire is the opposite of arrogance. Arrogant people aren't interested in learning because they think they already know it all and feel like they're above everything and everyone else.

A positive attitude generates positive waves and inspires others. We want to associate with people who don't dwell on the negative, stir up conflict, or see only problems. We prefer people who come to the table with a solution in hand. As we've already seen, at the end of a selection process, two or three people generally make the last cut. These individuals typically have similar profiles, and the factor that will tip the scales toward a given candidate is subjective and predominantly influenced by the enthusiasm, strength, and drive to do things well that each person demonstrates. This is what fuels a virtuous cycle of success. In the same way, it's important to be generous in handing out acceptance and approval. As we discussed earlier, everyone needs, at different levels, the acceptance and approval of others. The higher up on the ladder a person goes, the more acceptance and approval that person will require. It seems contradictory, but it's true. People with greater responsibilities and longer track records of success have bigger egos and, more than likely, need acceptance and approval more than others. And we need to give everyone what they need. We tend to wait for others to approve of us first before offering our approval. But the strategy that we recommend at Lee Hecht Harrison is just the opposite. We need to approve of and accept others first. If we make people feel good about themselves, then they reciprocate, and we are quickly on our way to establishing a wonderful relationship that generates a lasting bond based on trust.

How can we develop *chemistry*? The best way is to attend all of our meetings having previously made the personal decision to immediately give others our acceptance and approval. This helps ensure that the person sitting across from us feels good and is inclined to return the feeling. You can try the opposite. Go up to people and give them a dirty look, show your disapproval, make sure they know you don't accept them, ignore them, look down on them, and, immediately and intuitively, they will treat you in the same way. So, generously giving acceptance and approval works 100 percent in our favor. The more we give, the more we receive. This is called the law of reciprocity, which Keith Ferrazzi mentions in his book *Never Eat Alone*.[23]

. . . .

Follow this spiritual teaching: "Love your neighbor as you love yourself." Give what you wish to receive from others, and they will give you the same in return.

. . . .

I don't want this to sound like this approach is only a strategy to get what we want in business. That would be manipulative, and others see right through this. The acceptance and approval that we give should be honest and genuine. It's the only way to guarantee that the positive vibes we transmit to others are in fact well received. It's also an excellent way of coexisting with others and effectively managing our personal lives, as well as a great way of showing our success and security. It also allows us to give to others what we most desire for ourselves, whether we are conscious of it or not. We should always remember that people like us for the way we make them feel about themselves.

PROJECT AN IMAGE OF SUCCESS

As we've discussed, we need to make a conscious effort to develop our own halo of success by developing a clear idea of the image we hold of ourselves. Our image is the reflection of what we believe we are and we are the image of what we hope to become. How others see us is based on the answer we give to this question: "Do I feel successful?"

There is an enormous difference between working with people who come to work because they need to pay the bills or because they have no other choice and working with people who love what they do and want to grow, learn, and contribute. As Keith Ferrazzi said, "The real winners—those with astounding careers, warm relationships, and unstoppable charisma—are those people who put it all out there and don't waste a bunch of time and energy trying to be something (or someone) they're not. Charm is simply a matter of being yourself. Your uniqueness is your power."[24]

OWN YOUR ATTITUDE

We may not be able to change the way we look, but we can change the expression that we wear. Many times, people are unaware of the power in their facial expressions and body language. **We own our attitudes—the attitude we decide to have toward work, the one we choose to have toward life, and the attitude that truly defines our personal image.**

Let me share a personal story with you. Some time ago, at 25, one of my daughters got breast cancer. During the first year of the illness, the family remained united and optimistic while she received treatment from the best doctors at MD Anderson Cancer Center in Houston, Texas. We trusted that everything would go well. My daughter was very brave, and she went through the terrible process of chemotherapy, operations, and radiation with a very good and courageous attitude.

But the following year, the cancer came back, and it caught us off guard. I fell apart and terror took a hold of me. Unlike the year before, where I radiated positivity and transmitted hope to my daughter and the whole family, I walked around with a sadness that overwhelmed me— completely focused on my despair.

One night, my daughter told me softly, "Mom, you know that I love you very much, and that I appreciate everything you've done for me and for everyone else during all this time. But, I want to ask you something, and I hope you don't get mad. Mom, can you please change the expression on your face?"

I was completely taken aback. I didn't know what she was talking about. So, I asked, "What expression?"

She answered, "That one—the one that tells me that I'm going to die, that there's no hope for me, that there is no point in my fighting because I've already lost the battle."

It was only then that I realized how my face had only been transmitting negative messages to her, and that they had been making her feel very bad. So, I did the only thing I could do: I took a deep breath, tried to keep a good attitude, and changed the look on my face. Not only was it good for her, for the family, and for me, but I learned that with the right kind of motivation, it's possible to change our attitude in an instant, and that our face is good not only for expressing our emotions, but also for giving people feedback about themselves.

Thank God that our story had a happy ending. My daughter has been very well for seven years now. Currently, she is living in Manly Beach near Sydney, Australia.

If we continuously assess the messages our faces convey, then we can be aware of how we make others feel when they are with us. As Jack Welch says, leadership is about them, not us.[25]

SELL YOUR ENTHUSIASM

Imagine for a moment that you are living and working alone in a remote location. Your home is 50 miles away from the nearest town. You decide you want to find someone to share your life with. However, your prospects for finding a significant other, if you stay home alone, are pretty much limited to the UPS person who comes out occasionally. You need to get out of the house and, as they say in marketing, put yourself out there.

The next Saturday, there's a party in town. Obviously, you want to look nicer than you normally do working at home. When you arrive at the party, you don't know many people because you haven't been into town much. So you're faced with the following options: standing in the corner alone, or standing by the DJ making conversation. Clearly, the second approach is best, because if guests see that you're excited, smiling, and having a good time chatting with others, then more than one person will notice you. Here is the message that others from town will glean from this second approach:

- You went to the party; therefore, you exist.
- You're open to possibilities.
- You look like you want to dance.
- They see you dance, and you look like a fun person to know.

By going to parties, you get to know several people from

town, and you increase your possibilities of finding someone you really like. It's the same story on the job front.

Sometimes when people are at work, they seclude themselves in their offices. They don't go out, and they refuse
to attend events because they think it isn't necessary. They
make few connections because they're not out meeting
people and *showing* that they're ready to be pleasant, polite,
and good company. Hiding in the corner is not an effective
strategy for interacting with people.

Instead, we need to make sure that we radiate energy,
smile, are friendly, use a warm tone, and send the clear message that we're open to meeting new people. Charisma is
nothing more than positively managing our energy.

....

By positively managing our energy, we transmit that
positive energy to others. This is charisma: infecting
others with our enthusiasm.

....

When we are pleasant, positive, charismatic, and down
to earth in our professional lives, we project a successful
image. And if we feel successful, we'll be treated accordingly.
This is the power of attitude. Showing our successful side
does not involve bragging, being arrogant, or acting like
we're better than others. On the contrary, it simply means
understanding that our attitude has to be totally positive and
directed at giving others the attention and recognition that
they expect and possibly need. And what sells more than

offering excellent professional services that translate into enthusiasm as well as desire to keep learning and staying involved? The point is to try to win people's trust. If we're warm, authentic, and open, others will follow our lead. It isn't about impressing people. It's about making the connection that will lead to trust; and warmth is the energy that facilitates trust and openness.

DEVELOP CONTACTS AND RELATIONSHIPS

We've discussed how, as sales manager for You, Incorporated, our primary job is to sell our services, hire a good sales force, intimately understand our product, and believe in it. For this, we need contacts and relationships.

Why do we need to build and nurture our network of contacts? In the past, when jobs were safe forever, towns were small, and everyone knew everyone else, no one had to worry about developing a network of contacts. People didn't need to go out of their way to meet others or be careful about what image they projected.

As we've already discussed, things have drastically changed since then. Today, a network of contacts is a fundamental tool to sell our professional services. Herminia Ibarra, author of *Working Identity: Unconventional Strategies for Reinventing Your Career*,[26] summarizes the three components of a successful professional career in a diagram she uses in her presentations.

Skills, Knowledge, Achievements, and Results

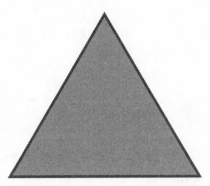

Image and Reputation   Contacts and Relationships

When many people hear the word *contact*, they think that building their contact network is just an elegant form of manipulation. It sounds like something people do solely to further their interests, and that once they get what they need from someone, they can sever that tie for good. This seems self-serving and unsavory. That's why I prefer to talk about networks of trust. Jeffrey Gitomer, author of *Little Black Book of Connections*, says, "All things being equal, people want to do business with their friends. All things being not quite equal, people STILL want to do business with their friends."[27] That is, people want to do business with others whom they know they can trust.

BUILD A NETWORK OF TRUST

What is a network of trust? It's the product of a conscious and voluntary effort to establish and maintain genuine, long-term contact with people who know and appreciate us and whom we appreciate back. Today, the majority of jobs are found through networking. When a job opens up, companies first look informally within the organization or to friends or clients. In fact, close to 90 percent of job openings are in what we call *the market of hidden opportunities.*[28]

....

Building a network of trust requires establishing long-term relationships with people who appreciate us and whom we appreciate back. These are people we have worked with or know well, with whom we keep a relationship based on trust, appreciation, and mutual respect.

....

The larger the network of trust we have, the likelier it is that we will have more opportunities to sell our services, because our contacts are our best salespeople and the best ones to speak well of our reputation. *Developing networks of trust requires having a clear idea of who our acquaintances are and what they know about us.* Remember, it's people, when asked for a reference, who will say either that you are "top-notch," or the opposite: "Don't even think about doing business together."

The first step in generating our network of trust entails making an organized list. Most of us have a network of between 300 to 500 people, but few of us have an organized list or are even aware that we have so many contacts. We can start by listing all the people we know and who know us, even if we haven't seen them for a while, and by taking into account the following groups of people:

- Friends and their families and acquaintances
- People we went to school and college with
- Blood relatives, in-laws, and their friends
- Mentors and key professional contacts
- Coworkers and former coworkers
- People we know from the club, gym, neighborhood, church, and professional organizations (and their relatives and acquaintances)
- Suppliers, clients, former suppliers, and former clients
- Relationships we may have formed at work with competitors or service providers
- Our children's friends' parents
- Lawyers, doctors, bankers, and so on

In other words, our list should include everyone who has hopefully formed a good impression of us since all of them have an influence over our reputation.

It's therefore in our best interest to make sure these people have a positive image of us regardless of the position they might occupy. Some people think that only influential people should be included in the network of trust, but as we will see later on, this is a mistake. My list of contacts has information on some 2,500 people, not only those whom I work with, but also those whom I've shared part of my life with or those whom I have contact with in the different circles in which I move. I have information on people at my office, friends from school, my doctor—even an infectious disease specialist (I got chickenpox as an adult)—the nice woman who works at the bank, my clients, the people I've directly helped find new jobs, my attorney friends, and so on. I have a copy of this list on my computer and my mobile phone, and I also back it up in the cloud. I always take time to update this list because it's an essential part of my livelihood.

A while back, when I was visiting a friend who was sick, a hospital administrator gave me a good piece of advice: "Always keep your list of trusted medical physicians updated because you never know when you might need it. If there's an emergency in the family, you will know just whom to call." I'm glad I listened to her advice and put it together. I now have more than 50 names of reputable doctors in different parts of the world, and the list has been useful not only to me but also my friends and acquaintances.

How can we develop a network of trust? Obviously, we need to keep our relationships current by continually updating our contacts. We also need to let these people know what's going on in our personal and professional lives. We should provide updates whenever we get promoted, learn something significant in our lives, fall down and manage to get back up, and so on. We also need to know what's going on with our contacts in terms of *their* personal lives, interests, and achievements. It's important to ask about these things with genuine interest. Remember that building networks of trust means re-establishing and rewriting the relationship in new terms and keeping it current. This also entails enthusiastically re-establishing our identity, image, and reputation with our contacts. It means constantly renewing our ties, even if we haven't seen each other in a while!

In this regard, social media, LinkedIn, Facebook Messanger, WhatsApp, and many other tools have made life much easier. Social networks allow us to stay connected with what's currently going on in other peoples' lives and ensure that they know what's going on in ours. Within the network of trust, we need to give a great deal of ourselves, but we must also keep one thing in mind: we must give to others what they may need. If we do this, we constantly rewrite our relationship and build a win-win relationship for everyone involved. If we keep our contacts up to date, we can better understand where people are in their own lives.

Let me give you an example. I have a friend from college who used to pass by my office from time to time. He drove a car from the 1970s that was always dirty, dented, and in need of maintenance. Every time I saw him drive by, I thought that things must not have gone well for him in life. One day, however, I saw him at a wedding, and I finally sat down to speak with him after almost 20 years. He may not have had much money, but he certainly was happy and pleasant. In fact, he was a great guy. He was intelligent, he was cultured, and he had a wonderful marriage and four children. This man was completely satisfied with his life. A stereotype—or perhaps prejudice—had led me to believe that he wasn't doing well because of the appearance of his car, but after reconnecting with him, I had the opportunity to get to know the real person beyond the image he was projecting through that beat-up, old vehicle.

Unfortunately, we live in a highly visual world where lots of images flash quickly before our eyes. We are forced to quickly classify these mental photos somewhere within our brains. Without much thought, we place these images in *boxes* or mental categories. For example, we assign an old and poorly kept car to *failure*, and a clean, new car to *success*. As a result, we end up passing judgment on people, sometimes mistakenly.

We build our network of trust by keeping up to date with others and inquiring about their lives. Why? To maintain ties with others and bring positive things to them.

RECOGNIZE THAT NO CONTACT IS TOO SMALL

One of the many mistakes we can make when creating our network of trust—one that stands out as particularly perverse—is believing that there are small and unimportant contacts. Some people sneer at others and believe that their list of contacts should only include those friends who are general managers at banks or relatives in high-ranking positions. These people tend to neglect their ties and relationships with people who are at different levels than their own. They also insist that if *so and so* doesn't have a highly visible job or *hasn't done very well*, it's useless to include that person in their network of trust.

In fact, not too long ago I was helping someone create a list of contacts, and he said, "I'm not going to put people from school on the list because they haven't done anything with their lives."

I answered, "So? Remember, you may know what they do, but you don't know who they know."

Always beware of preconceived notions.

I have a great story from our office in Peru. Two brothers earned their living by waxing cars in our company's parking lot, and sometimes our clients would ask the brothers to wax their car while they met with us. One such client, who was an executive going through a job transition process, finished his meeting with us earlier than expected, and the brothers hadn't finished waxing his car. The brothers started to talk to our client while they finished their work. They knew what we do at Lee Hecht Harrison, so they asked him, "And what are you up to? Are you in the process of relocating?"

The executive told them that he was a marketing expert. He explained, "I've worked as a manager at a firm, and now I am in the process of building my network of trust and looking at available opportunities."

"Look, we also wax cars at another company," one of the brothers told him. "One of our clients there was also a marketing manager. He recently left because he took a job at another firm. I think he went to the competition, but I am not certain. In any case, if he isn't there anymore, they must be looking to replace him. Maybe there's a job opening."

Our candidate took note, looked within his contact list for someone in that organization, and set up a meeting. He didn't open the meeting by saying something like, "Hi, I know there's a job opening here, and I need it." Instead, he went prepared with a list of information to share with the people who interviewed him, including the value he could add to their company. As a result, he interested the hiring managers, and he became a real contender for the job. Ultimately, he landed the job, and he has been working there for a while now.

....

> There's no such thing as a small contact—we should never underestimate the power of any connection.

....

We now know that as many as nine out of 10 positions are filled through contacts and connections.[29] This is a world of word-of-mouth references, as I mentioned earlier. People typically don't look in the yellow pages for a surgeon to operate on their gallbladder or find an attorney through an Internet ad.

At our seminars, we often ask, "How many of you have gotten your position through contacts?" Close to 90 percent of participants answer "yes" to this question. As another example, one of our clients, an executive, went to the dentist to be treated for a cavity. During that office visit, he explained to the dentist that he was in the middle of a job transition process and that he was excited about the prospect of relocating and improving his employability.

His dentist said, "I have a patient who's retiring. He is looking for his replacement at his laboratory; maybe that could be you."

The dentist put the two in contact with each other, and things went smoothly. Today, our client is general manager at this pharmaceutical laboratory.

Keeping all of this in mind, *it's important to remember that finding a position through contacts isn't the same as having someone forcibly exert their influence to get us a job.* It means we find out about a job opening through one of our contacts and/or we are recommended for a particular position by someone in our network of trust. This is what it means to build and nurture our network.

Whenever we attend an event, we should spend 25 percent of our time with people we know and the rest of the time getting to know new people. However, this is often difficult for us to do. Do you know why? Because human beings are sociable by nature, but at the same time, the older they become, the harder it is for them to accept new things (and this includes new people). Consequently, you need to practice and develop this skill. Always remember to take your business cards with you to hand out to the people you meet. Hopefully these people will become new connections within your network of trust.

BUILD TIES BEFORE YOU NEED THEM

Many people decide to build their network of trust when they think they're about to lose their jobs. They begin to tell friends, "Hey, I'm updating my résumé because I may lose my job. I'll send it to you." But by then, it's too late. Besides, the network of contacts shouldn't be used like this. It's a network of trust, and as such, it's a long-term effort. It needs to be built over time.

Where should we direct our efforts? Everywhere! Social gatherings, work events, committees, seminars, courses, work meetings, trips, the gym, weddings, parents' associations, professional association events, sporting events, and so on. Human beings are highly social. No one's saying that we need to go to every event we're invited to, but we have to keep in mind that social or professional events and day-to-day activities provide the perfect chance to tell others what we're doing and find out what's going on with them. Relating with others is important because it shows that we have a genuine interest in them.

DON'T DISAPPEAR FROM THE SCENE

As professionals, our reputation would hit rock bottom if someone asked, "What happened to him?" or "What happened to her?" and no one knew because they hadn't seen or heard from us in ages. This would mean that no one really knows us. If we make a living by selling our professional services, then we need to remain visible at all times. *The day we disappear, so does our business.* This comes with the territory—professionals, executives, lawyers, doctors, engineers, administrators, economists, technicians, office workers, entrepreneurs, independent contractors—all of us who make a living out of selling our services or are self-employed must always remain visible. No one can afford to hide. Developing and maintaining our network of trust is an ongoing activity.

MANAGE YOUR PERSONAL BRAND IN SOCIAL NETWORKS

One of the main excuses for not building networks of trust is lacking the time it takes to do it. However, today social media platforms such as LinkedIn, Twitter, or Facebook help us quickly stay connected even when we're short on time. Here are a few ideas about how to handle our personal brand within social media.

1. *We should be very careful about what we publish and where we publish it.* What goes around comes around, and we should pay attention to what we publish and how we show up in social media. Whatever is posted—by you or others—will stay out there forever.

2. *We need to frequently review what appears about us on the web, because we're there whether we like it or not.* Everyone—including human resource managers and headhunters—uses the internet to research their interview candidates. They carefully review all of the material they find, including, of course, photographs. We need to be sure that we have an impeccable record that is consistent with our professional image.

   We did a study at Lee Hecht Harrison in Peru in December 2014 with a sample of 1,360 executives.[30] We found that 90 percent of the executives surveyed believed that social media was used to search for talent,[31] and 56 percent[32] affirmed having used social media for this purpose. This number was significantly higher among human resource executives, where 80 percent said they had used social media to search for talent.[33] And in terms of references, 67 percent of all executives asserted that they had looked for information about candidates through social media. The percentage is greater among HR executives, as 80 percent confirmed having used the web for this purpose.[34] Ninety percent of this group looked for references on LinkedIn, 59 percent searched Facebook for information about candidates, and 9 percent looked for information on Twitter.[35] It's important to note that in the case of LinkedIn, 88 percent of the information found had a positive influence on those who were looking to hire, but in the case of Facebook, this percentage fell considerably—to 56 percent—because 44 percent of the information found was deemed negative.[36]

That's right, negative! Many people think that what they write and share on social media is private and safe information that can only be viewed by their *friends*. In fact, social media is a very public arena in which everything we do and say about others and ourselves may be on display. Remember that all the information on social media may be read and interpreted in one way or another by people who are seeking to learn about our values, behavior, and conduct at any point. These networks have virtually erased the fine line between what's public and private and between our personal and professional lives.

3. *We need to keep our profiles updated.* It's a good idea to be present in a professional network such as LinkedIn and to have control over the information that search engines reveal about us. Carefully fill out your profile and upload your résumé, then review the information periodically to make sure it's up to date. Ideally, you should review or update this information every month.

4. *For professional purposes, it's best to have an email address that is serious and formal.* Failing to do so doesn't make a good impression. For example, how would you like to receive a message from *thecobra77@hotmail.com?*

....

Summarizing, we need to continuously review the information about us and our personal brand on the Internet, and ensure it matches the image we want to project.

....

OVERCOME BARRIERS

As we've discussed, *we need to take advantage of all the opportunities that we have to update our network of contacts by attending courses, seminars, trips, and social activities. Each event gives us a chance to meet new people and show what we're about.* The idea is to start by interacting with more people than we usually do. This requires leaving our comfort zone and going out on a limb to meet new people.

How should we initiate contact? Let's say that we're at an event and we want to take advantage of the opportunity to meet new people. The idea is to look for things that we have in common with others. In most cases, if we're all at the same event, then we must have something in common.

. . . .

Before we start talking about ourselves we should show real interest in others. Remember to listen.

. . . .

Try to remember the name of the person you're chatting with, and mention it in the course of conversation. This will show the other person that you're paying attention and are genuinely interested in what he or she has to say.

Remember to be positive. Avoid discussing your problems: our contacts are not our psychotherapists! It's also not wise to speak poorly of others. This only serves to drive people away. Everyone wants to be involved with positive people who spread happiness and help them feel good. Start by trying to convey sincere and honest appreciation for others.

CREATE AN ACTION PLAN FOR SUCCESS

To achieve success in You, Incorporated, what do we need to do? *We need to generate clear and obvious results.* We now know that we're not paid to go to work; we're paid to do something specific, and we must have a clear idea of what this is and how it will be measured. Remember, we're paid to generate results and add value. *We need to know what our market value is and how we can contribute to the market and the industry.*

....

Changes provide a wonderful opportunity to advance our careers.

....

Change provides the perfect chance to show what we're made of and whether we're capable of courageously facing and navigating new scenarios while leading and helping others ride the wave of change. During changes, we can't forget about others. We need to know how people are managing, identify their challenges, and help them move forward. Also, we need to try to understand that in every change, the circles of power and decision-makers change the way they interact with each other, and these changing interactions may impact us and our networks of trust in myriad ways.

Productive visibility is important. We already know that we can't disappear. On the contrary, we need to be out there "mingling" to make sure that people know we exist and are aware of our achievements by communicating in a warm and down-to-earth way—not arrogantly. We need to maintain a winning and enthusiastic attitude that transmits energy and clearly shows that we know where we're going and how we're going to get there. We need to constantly monitor our progress. We need to ask ourselves, "Am I doing well?" and "Am I making progress?" It is also vital to constantly check if the competition is catching up to us.

We also need mentors to watch over our careers and to listen to our concerns. These people will not only help us, but will also give us a good reality check if we need one. I have nine mentors, all of whom I visit regularly, at least once a year. On these visits, I ask them to tell me how I'm doing, and I listen to their advice.

In terms of communication skills, we have seen how important it is to synthesize information and speak solidly in public.

....

Classes and seminars are vital because we must keep learning and doing so faster.

....

There are two rules: 1) Make contacts, contacts, and more contacts, and 2) always have your résumé updated. Your résumé isn't just a tool to find a job; it's also a way for you to monitor your career advancement. An up-to-date résumé helps us identify what we're contributing, what we have learned, and what progress we've made. It's our personal career advancement tool, and we need to use it well.

AS WE WRAP UP, LET'S REMEMBER...

- We don't have an intrinsic right to a job: we have to earn it over and over again with each passing day.
- We're not paid to go to work. We are paid to provide services that add value and generate results.
- Our security is derived from our level of employability and our willingness to ensure that we are up to date and competitive.
- Our success depends greatly upon our values, our performance, reputation and personal brand, the passion we work with, and the skills we develop along the way.
- We need to aspire to be successful people and professionals, without guilt or apologies.
- We must implement our professional plans in a very responsible and adult way and understand that no matter what our position may be, we are service providers and therefore we are in control of our career.
- Regardless of the type of relationships we have with our clients and bosses, we need to maintain a good attitude when providing our services.

To summarize, the following people are successful:

- Those who understand the reality of the new working world.
- Those who know what they want, set specific goals, and prepare in order to achieve them.

- Those who dare to dream of success.
- Those who are ethical in all circumstances.
- Those who have contacts and a good network of trust.
- Those who preserve and develop their personal brand and reputation.
- Those who generate quantifiable results.
- Those who develop their charisma, authenticity, and warmth.

· ·

As we can see, there's much to do, and a great deal of effort is required to be successful. But our dreams and aspirations are right in front of us, ripe for the taking. Dare to be successful!

· ·

To end this book, I would like to quote Henry David Thoreau, who left a positive mark on my life the first time I read his work. He continues to inspire me day after day with thoughts such as the following:

· ·

"Life isn't about finding yourself; it's about *creating* yourself."

· ·

For further reading see the infographic on page 161

EPILOGUE

I have much more to tell you about increasing your employability and improving your personal brand, expanding your network of contacts, treating your career development as your business, and many other things that can help you fulfill your professional and personal dreams. I hate to see it end here.

For those of you who would like more practical information on these topics and other related points, please visit my website at: *inestemple.com,* which has an archive with more than 750 free articles and short videos on developing your career and personal brand (in English and Spanish).

I have a fan page on Facebook that has much of this information at: facebook.com/InesTemple.Oficial.

You can also check out Lee Hecht Harrison's website: *lhh.com*

Or follow me on *Twitter*: @InesTemple

I wish you the best in your career and would like to leave you with a parting thought. Many years ago, I discovered that God also looks after us in our professional lives. I always ask Him to help me be the best driver of my career and help me improve as a person. You just need to ask for help with all your heart. After more than 25 years of experience in dealing with career issues, I have ample proof that God always helps us and never fails us, even if it just takes a while sometimes...

APPENDIX

ADDITIONAL RESOURCES

Chapter 1: The Only Constant Is Change

1. **The Stars of Our Reputation** http://www.inestemple.com/2016/07/the-stars-of-our-reputation/
2. **Attitude Matters when In a Job Transition** https://www.inestemple.com/2016/06/attitude-matters-when-in-a-job-transition/
3. **When is the Right Time to Change Jobs?** https://www.inestemple.com/2016/08/when-is-the-right-time-to-change-jobs/
4. **Do You Have A Plan B For Your Career?** https://www.inestemple.com/2018/03/do-you-have-a-plan-b-for-your-career/
5. **Is It Time to Change Jobs?** http://www.inestemple.com/2018/03/is-it-time-to-change-jobs/
6. **Your Career in the Digital Age** http://www.inestemple.com/2017/09/your-career-in-the-digital-age/
7. **Re-Examining Myths about Work** http://www.inestemple.com/2004/07/re-examining-myths-about-work/

Chapter 2: Employability

8. **Twelve Things That Good Leaders Do** http://www.inestemple.com/2015/04/twelve-things-that-good-leaders-do-2/
9. **Are You Treating Your People Badly?** http://www.inestemple.com/2016/10/are-you-treating-your-people-badly/

10. **Eight Ideas for Improving Our Employability** http://www
    .inestemple.com/2016/05/8-ideas-for-improving-employ
    ability/
11. **Leaders Who Inspire Me** http://www.inestemple.com/2016/
    08/the-leaders-who-inspire-me/
12. **Put Passion into What You Do** http://www.inestemple.com/
    2016/05/put-passion-into-what-you-do/
13. **Ten Ways to Display Your Talent** http://www.inestemple
    .com/2017/04/ten-ways-to-display-your-talent/
14. **Eight Ideas about Adversity** http://www.inestemple.com/
    2017/01/eight-ideas-about-adversity/

Chapter 3: Improving Your Personal Competitiveness

15. **Eleven Reasons Why You Would Be Fired** http://www
    .inestemple.com/2015/09/11-reasons-why-you-will-get-fired/
16. **Eleven Ways to Inspire** http://www.inestemple.com/2015/
    12/11-ways-to-inspire/
17. **Eleven More Things that Really Inspire Me** http://www
    .inestemple.com/2016/01/eleven-more-ways-to-inspire/
18. **How Well Do You Handle Your Interpersonal Relationships?**
    http://www.inestemple.com/2017/02/how-well-do-you
    -handle-your-interpersonal-relationships/
19. **The Value of Authenticity** http://www.inestemple.com/
    2016/06/the-value-of-authenticity/
20. **Learn Faster** http://www.inestemple.com/2016/09/learn-faster/
21. **Are you a Strategic Resource?** http://www.inestemple.com/
    2016/02/are-you-a-strategic-resource/
22. **Hacking Our Brain** http://www.inestemple.com/2018/01/
    hacking-our-brain/

Chapter 4: You, Incorporated

23. **Fourteen Mistakes That Will Make You Look Really Unprofessional to Your Boss** https://www.inestemple.com/2016/02/14-mistakes-in-the-professional-relationship-with-the-boss/

24. **Six Ways You May Be Sabotaging Your Career** http://www.inestemple.com/2016/10/six-ways-you-may-be-sabotaging-your-career/

25. **Your Name Is Your Brand, Take Care of It** http://www.inestemple.com/2014/06/your-name-is-your-brand-take-good-care-of-it/

26. **Eight Steps to Credibility** http://www.inestemple.com/2014/03/eight-steps-to-credibility/

27. **How to Destroy Your Career in A Few Steps** http://www.inestemple.com/2014/09/how-to-destroy-your-career-in-a-few-steps/

28. **How Do You Make Others Feel?** http://www.inestemple.com/2016/12/how-do-you-make-others-feel/

29. **Fifteen Things I Have Learned About Loyalty** https://www.inestemple.com/2016/03/15-things-i-have-learned-about-loyalty/

30. **What We Say About Ourselves** http://www.inestemple.com/2015/10/what-we-say-about-ourselves/

Chapter 5: Personal Marketing

31. **Ten Reasons You Weren't Hired** http://www.inestemple.com/2016/04/nine-reasons-you-didnt-get-hired/

32. **Nothing Sells Better Than Enthusiasm** https://www.inestemple.com/2018/06/nothing-sells-better-than-enthusiasm/

33. **Ten Serious Networking Mistakes** https://www.inestemple.com/2018/05/ten-serious-networking-mistakes/

34. **Reasons Why I Would Lose Trust In You** http://www.ines temple.com/2016/02/reasons-why-i-would-lose-trust-in-you/
35. **Mentors** http://www.inestemple.com/2014/12/mentors/
36. **Who Will Achieve Professional Success?** http://www.ines temple.com/2015/01/those-who-achieve-professional-success/
37. **Success Is the Best Revenge** http://www.inestemple.com/2015/01/success-is-the-best-revenge-2/
38. **Signs of a Poor Attitude at Work** http://www.inestemple.com/2014/08/signs-of-a-poor-attitude-at-work/
39. **Visualizing Your Success** http://www.inestemple.com/2016/02/visualizing-your-success/

Articles of Interest for Further Reading

40. **Inspiring Women** http://www.inestemple.com/2014/10/inspiring-women/
41. **Questions to Ask Ourselves** http://www.inestemple.com/2018/05/questions-to-ask-ourselves/
42. **Green with Envy** http://www.inestemple.com/2014/11/green-with-envy/
43. **Flee from Negative People!** http://www.inestemple.com/2013/09/flee-from-negativists/
44. **Twelve Things that Good Leaders Do** http://www.inestemple.com/2015/04/twelve-things-that-good-leaders-do-2/
45. **Communicate to Lead** http://www.inestemple.com/2014/05/communicate-to-lead/
46. **Stars of Your Personal Brand** http://www.inestemple.com/2018/05/stars-of-your-personal-brand/
47. **Ten Ideas for Your Personal Brand** http://www.inestemple.com/2012/02/10-ideas-for-your-personal-brand/
48. **Personal Brands and Social Media** http://www.inestemple.com/2018/05/personal-brands-and-social-media/

Additional Articles

49. **How to Resign with Class** https://www.inestemple.com/ 2018/02/how-to-resign-with-class/
50. **In Search of Professional Happiness** https://www.inestemple .com/2017/10/in-search-of-professional-happiness/
51. **The Power of Bouncing Back** https://www.inestemple.com/ 2017/07/the-power-of-bouncing-back/
52. **What Will Your Next Job Be?** https://www.inestemple.com/ 2015/06/what-will-your-next-job-be/
53. **The Best Way to Reposition Yourself after Losing Your Job** https://www.inestemple.com/2016/10/the-best-way-to-repo sition-yourself-after-losing-your-job/
54. **Outplacement as an Opportunity** https://www.inestemple .com/2016/10/outplacement-as-an-opportunity/
55. **My First Job** https://www.inestemple.com/2015/11/my-first -job/
56. **Change Your Perspective to Move Forward** https://www.ineste mple.com/2017/03/change-your-perspective-to-move-forward/
57. **Does Your Career Have A Road Map?** https://www .inestemple.com/2017/02/does-your-career-have-a-road-map/
58. **How Do I Make My Boss Happy with My Work?** https:// www.inestemple.com/2016/10/how-do-i-make-my-boss -happy-with-my-work/
59. **Beware of Elastic Ethics!** https://www.inestemple.com/2013/ 08/beware-of-elastic-ethics/
60. **I Want to Be an Entrepreneur!** https://www.inestemple.com/ 2014/08/i-want-to-be-an-entrepreneur/
61. **What I Wanted to Be When I Grew Up** https://www .inestemple.com/2012/09/what-i-wanted-to-be-when-i -grew-up/
62. **The Great Effects of Apologizing** https://www.inestemple .com/2016/10/the-great-impact-of-apologizing/

63. **What Progress Have You Made In Your Career Plan?** https://www.inestemple.com/2015/07/what-progress-have-you-made-in-your-career-plan/

64. **A Good Attitude Makes All the Difference** https://www.inestemple.com/2017/09/ua-good-attitude-makes-all-the-difference/

65. **Weaving Our Networks of Trust** https://www.inestemple.com/2014/07/weaving-our-networks-of-trust-2/

66. **Eleven Thoughts on the Ego in Success and Power** https://www.inestemple.com/2018/03/eleven-thoughts-on-the-ego-in-success-and-power/

67. **Online Personal Brand** https://www.inestemple.com/2015/09/online-personal-brand/

68. **Mentors and Mentees** https://www.inestemple.com/2016/11/mentors-and-mentees/

INFOGRAPHICS

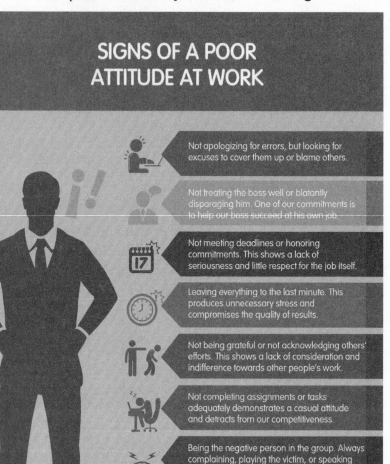

SIGNS OF A POOR ATTITUDE AT WORK

Not apologizing for errors, but looking for excuses to cover them up or blame others.

Not treating the boss well or blatantly disparaging him. One of our commitments is to help our boss succeed at his own job.

Not meeting deadlines or honoring commitments. This shows a lack of seriousness and little respect for the job itself.

Leaving everything to the last minute. This produces unnecessary stress and compromises the quality of results.

Not being grateful or not acknowledging others' efforts. This shows a lack of consideration and indifference towards other people's work.

Not completing assignments or tasks adequately demonstrates a casual attitude and detracts from our competitiveness.

Being the negative person in the group. Always complaining, playing the victim, or speaking badly of others makes us unpopular.

Not participating in office social events or not showing interest in the personal lives of others shows indifference and little team spirit.

Not paying attention at meetings but rather answering e-mails or texting reflects a lack of interest and bad manners.

LEE HECHT HARRISON | DBM

Author: Ines Temple / Design: Hashtag

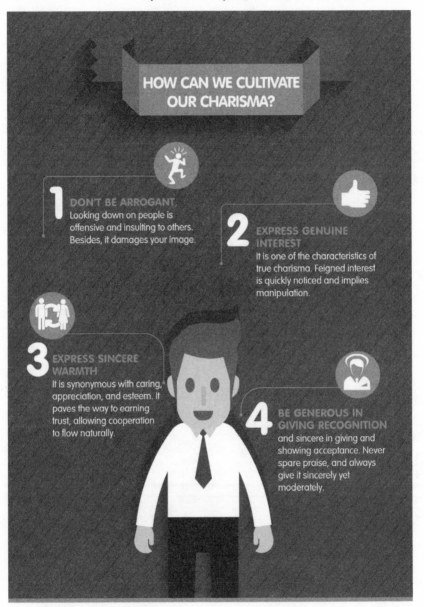

HOW CAN WE CULTIVATE OUR CHARISMA?

1 DON'T BE ARROGANT.
Looking down on people is offensive and insulting to others. Besides, it damages your image.

2 EXPRESS GENUINE INTEREST
It is one of the characteristics of true charisma. Feigned interest is quickly noticed and implies manipulation.

3 EXPRESS SINCERE WARMTH
It is synonymous with caring, appreciation, and esteem. It paves the way to earning trust, allowing cooperation to flow naturally.

4 BE GENEROUS IN GIVING RECOGNITION
and sincere in giving and showing acceptance. Never spare praise, and always give it sincerely yet moderately.

LEE HECHT HARRISON | DBM

Author: Ines Temple / Design: Hashtag

10 THINGS EMPLOYABLE PEOPLE DO NOT DO

1 They don't assume their job will last forever. They know that jobs last as long as they work for both parties.

2 They don't continually confront their boss. They accept their bosses as they are and treat them like their best clients.

3 They don't isolate or close themselves off. They understand that their networks of trust are vital.

4 They don't let themselves become outdated. They seek to learn, grow, and deepen their knowledge.

5 They don't leave things to chance. They are ambitious and they establish demanding goals.

6 They don't see themselves as an employee. They manage their career as if it were their best own business.

7 They don't wear a frown. They know that their charisma is key to building trust.

8 They don't try to make the least possible effort. They take a real interest in what they do and do more than what they are asked.

9 They don't neglect their personal brand. They act with integrity in every aspect of their life.

10 They don't live scheming. They are open, share knowledge, friendships, and information.

LEE HECHT HARRISON | DBM

Author: Ines Temple / Design: Hashtag

158

SEVEN SINS AGAINST YOUR PERSONAL BRAND

Your name is your lifetime brand and it is in your best interest to take care of it. However, here are seven sins you can commit against your personal brand.

1 ARROGANCE

Nothing can justify arrogance; not a career full of promotions and achievements, not a flawless academic education, not success, power, and fortune, not even great looks.

2 COMPLACENCY

Whoever falls into complacency forgets that all jobs are temporary and that each of us is solely responsible for the success and relevance of our brand.

3 UNETHICAL CONDUCT

Unethical people do business while having conflicts of interest; they deceive and lie to everyone, have no word, and do no respect others.

4 BAD RESULTS, FEW ACHIEVEMENTS

A lack of tenacity or purpose, or not meeting the agreed success indicators, irreparably affects our resume, our brand, and our professional reputation.

5 NEGLECTING OUR PERSONAL IMAGE

Bad habits, addictions, messy appearance, lack of exercise or hygiene, and improper language all have a very negative effect on our brand.

6 FEW CONTACTS

A lack of interest in others or indifference towards co-workers leads to self-isolation and a small and potentially poor network of trust.

7 BAD ATTITUDE

A negative, fault-finding, or selfish person who does not care if others are satisfied at work or who fails to give recognition to his or her people rarely has a good image or reputation.

LEE HECHT HARRISON | DBM

Author: Ines Temple / Design: Hashtag

THREE GOOD IDEAS TO BOOST YOUR CAREER

We must take care of our personal brand with our co-workers, because they are the ones who get to know us and who can make or unmake our reputation without a second thought.

1 BUILD DIFFERENTIATING SKILLS

This produces achievements and results, and adds clear and evident value. It is also important to develop clear and empathic leadership skills to lead change and develop teams.

2 BUILD NETWORKS OF TRUST

Many people focus on doing their job well and learning new skills; others assume that contacts are only useful when they are looking for a job. Networks of trust open the doors to better opportunities for obtaining ideas, support, and resources.

3 TAKE CARE OF YOUR PERSONAL BRAND

Our professional reputation is the best letter of presentation we have. It is the impression we give others about our efforts, reliability, passion for work, and attitude that makes the difference, and is remembered by others.

LEE HECHT HARRISON | DBM

Author: Ines Temple / Design: Hashtag

EIGHT STEPS TO CREDIBILITY

01

Those who value their credibility **act in accordance with their values and principles,** without yielding to the temptation of immediate gain, because they know that trust is the basis for reputation and prestige.

02

They do not oversell themselves, nor do they indulge in self-promotion, because their credibility is based on realities and not just on appearances.

03

They do not improvise or rest on their laurels. They are serious, dedicated, and disciplined, and you can rely on them because they prepare well to practice their specialty.

04

They keep their word and honor their promises and commitments. They do not retract themselves or change their minds lightly, and they do not need signed papers to validate their agreements.

05

They are consistent, they uphold the same values for their personal and professional lives, without double standards. They are people of integrity and live without conflicts of interest or of ethics.

06

They are loyal even in hard times. They do not sell their loyalties to the highest bidder or tarnish the reputation of others through gossip.

07

They give credit where it is due and never take credit for the merits of others. They do not plagiarize or copy anyone else's intellectual work. They publicly thank others for their contributions.

08

They tell the truth. They tend to be opinion leaders who do not stop doing what is right, even when it makes them temporarily unpopular. They are honest and transparent.

LEE HECHT HARRISON | **DBM**

Author: Ines Temple / Design: Hashtag

How to Destroy Your Career in a Few Steps

Things you should never do if you want to take good care of your career and your personal brand.

Forget subtlety, tell your bosses, your clients, and your coworkers what you really think of them. Don't worry about maintaining your network of trust, because that's for people with nothing better to do.

Lie about everything, do not worry about the fact that everything can be verified on the Internet. If you can, bribe people, everyone does it, right? And all that stuff about keeping your word, like watching your credibility and your good reputation, is outdated.

Make sure everyone knows you are better than them, if you already feel relatively successful at your job, stop worrying about developing yourself, learning new things, reading, and attending courses.

Forget about any indicators of success of your position, or anything else related to adding value or doing things well. The idea is to survive every boss and every change in the organization.

Take credit for your team's successes, do not try to develop your people, because then they could reduce your merits or, even worse, take your job.

Bring your personal problems to the office. Use Facebook so that your friends know everything that is going on at your office, what you think about your co-workers, and especially about your boss.

LEE HECHT HARRISON | DBM

Author: Ines Temple / Design: Hashtag

163

PERSONAL MARKETING TIPS

 1 All jobs are temporary and last as long as they work for both, the companies and employees.

 2 We have to find satisfaction in our current position and not what lies down the road, such as a promotion or a raise.

 3 There is nothing better than enjoying our work. This leads to working better and becoming more involved.

 4 We have to take care of our attitude towards both internal and external clients and remember that our main client is our boss.

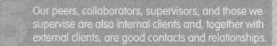 **5** Our peers, collaborators, supervisors, and those we supervise are also internal clients and, together with external clients, are good contacts and relationships.

 6 To be more employable, we must do more than what is asked of us, which means adding our own contributions, not improvising, and improving each day.

 7 Our attitude is vital for success. The passion we put into our work determines our employability level.

LEE HECHT HARRISON | DBM

Author: Ines Temple / Design: Hashtag

Who Achieves Professional Success

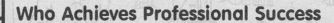

1

Those who really understand the working world: We will be "job-attractive" when we add value and produce concrete achievements.

2

Those who know what they want and are prepared to achieve it: Only people with clear objectives are successful.

3

Those who are ethical: The working world does not excuse or forget those who break their word or are unethical.

4

Those who have contacts: A contact network is a fundamental tool for consistently "selling" the quality of our professional services.

5

Those who take care of their brand and reputation: Successful people actively tend to their image and reputation to keep themselves competitive and employable.

6

Those who produce results: We are not paid to go to work, but to add value, to contribute to results, and to meet objectives and specific goals.

7

Those who develop their charisma: For people to trust us, we must begin by creating a warm and genuine bond, and that fosters trust (Charisma = Warmth).

LEE HECHT HARRISON | DBM

Author: Ines Temple / Design: Hashtag

165

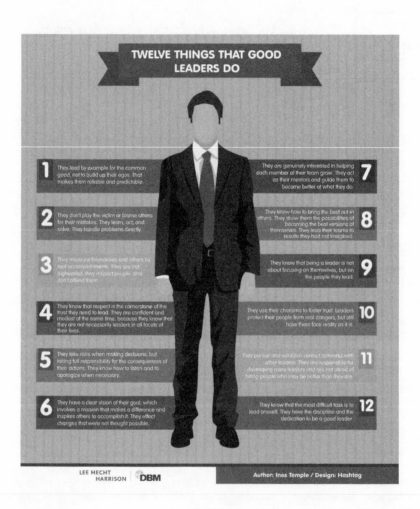

TWELVE THINGS THAT GOOD LEADERS DO

1 They lead by example for the common good, not to build up their egos. That makes them reliable and predictable.

2 They don't play the victim or blame others for their mistakes. They learn, act, and solve. They handle problems directly.

3 They measure themselves and others by real accomplishments. They are not bigheaded, they respect people, and don't offend them.

4 They know that respect is the cornerstone of the trust they need to lead. They are confident and modest at the same time, because they know that they are not necessarily leaders in all facets of their lives.

5 They take risks when making decisions, but taking full responsibility for the consequences of their actions. They know how to listen and to apologize when necessary.

6 They have a clear vision of their goal, which involves a mission that makes a difference and inspires others to accomplish it. They effect changes that were not thought possible.

7 They are genuinely interested in helping each member of their team grow. They act as their mentors and guide them to become better at what they do.

8 They know how to bring the best out in others. They show them the possibilities of becoming the best versions of themselves. They lead their teams to results they had not imagined.

9 They know that being a leader is not about focusing on themselves, but on the people they lead.

10 They use their charisma to foster trust. Leaders protect their people from real dangers, but still have them face reality as it is.

11 They pursue and establish contact networks with other leaders. They are responsible for developing more leaders and are not afraid of hiring people who may be better than they are.

12 They know that the most difficult task is to lead oneself. They have the discipline and the dedication to be a good leader.

LEE HECHT HARRISON **DBM**

Author: Ines Temple / Design: Hashtag

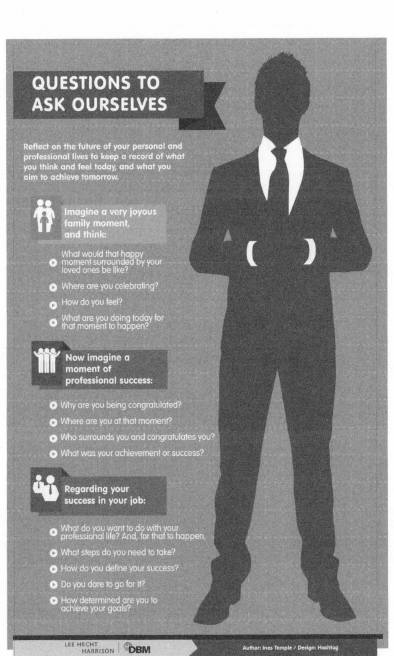

QUESTIONS TO ASK OURSELVES

Reflect on the future of your personal and professional lives to keep a record of what you think and feel today, and what you aim to achieve tomorrow.

Imagine a very joyous family moment, and think:

- What would that happy moment surrounded by your loved ones be like?
- Where are you celebrating?
- How do you feel?
- What are you doing today for that moment to happen?

Now imagine a moment of professional success:

- Why are you being congratulated?
- Where are you at that moment?
- Who surrounds you and congratulates you?
- What was your achievement or success?

Regarding your success in your job:

- What do you want to do with your professional life? And, for that to happen,
- What steps do you need to take?
- How do you define your success?
- Do you dare to go for it?
- How determined are you to achieve your goals?

LEE HECHT HARRISON | DBM

Author: Ines Temple / Design: Hashtag

167

IMPROVING OUR EMPLOYABILITY

The more employable we are, the more demand there will be for our services, and the better our opportunities. There are three areas to work on to be more employable:

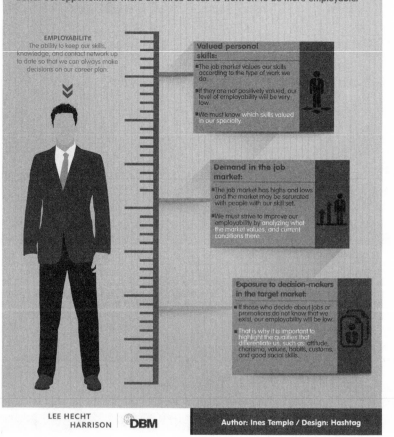

EMPLOYABILITY:
The ability to keep our skills, knowledge, and contact network up to date so that we can always make decisions on our career plan.

Valued personal skills:
- The job market values our skills according to the type of work we do.
- If they are not positively valued, our level of employability will be very low.
- We must know which skills valued in our specialty.

Demand in the job market:
- The job market has highs and lows and the market may be saturated with people with our skill set.
- We must strive to improve our employability by analyzing what the market values, and current conditions there.

Exposure to decision-makers in the target market:
- If those who decide about jobs or promotions do not know that we exist, our employability will be low.
- That is why it is important to highlight the qualities that differentiate us, such as: attitude, charisma, values, habits, customs, and good social skills.

LEE HECHT HARRISON | **DBM**

Author: Ines Temple / Design: Hashtag

168

YOUR NAME IS YOUR BRAND, TAKE CARE OF IT

01 ▷ Our name is our personal brand for life –present wherever we go–, and it is in our best interest to take care of it.

02 ▷ A good reputation is always earned with honest effort, without shortcuts, and is upheld over time by means of integrity, ethics, and values.

03 ▷ We need to maintain a good relationship with everyone we can, not make enemies since they will affect the perceived value of our brand.

04 It is a good idea to regularly appraise the standing of our name and reputation. We represent our brand every day, so we must always act with integrity, and not only in our professional lives.

05 ▷ We must be committed to our brand, since our responsibility for taking care of it never ends. Our name is our brand for life and a good reputation **helps us enhance our employability!**

LEE HECHT HARRISON | DBM

Author: Ines Temple / Design: Hashtag

STARS FOR YOUR PERSONAL BRAND

How our clients experience our services is a result of our life mission and a well-developed career plan.

It depends on our service attitude to understand the needs of our clients and on the results we deliver.

We need to work for this, but it will build our reputation and increase the value of our personal brand over time.

1 THE SELF-EMPLOYED

They know that their professional success is directly related to their service mission, the results they deliver, and the quality of service they provide. They know that the better their reputation and prestige, the more clients they will have.

2 ENTREPRENEURS

They too know this. They rely on their good name, ethics, and prestige to win the loyalty of their clients. Clients recognize when companies base their its strategy on customer satisfaction more than on profits.

3 EMPLOYEES

We have a single client who pays us on a regular basis. This leads us to feel a false sense of professional security. So, we must not forget that our career depends on our prestige and on satisfying our client!

LEE HECHT HARRISON · DBM

Author: Ines Temple / Design: Hashtag

INTEGRITY, ETHICS, AND VALUES

It is essential to build our personal brand on values and ethics. Together with integrity, they are the cornerstones of reputation.

It is better to protect our employers, partners, and contacts' trust. Our good name endures when based on integrity, ethics and values.

We all have a personal brand to take care of, and a good reputation is earned with honest effort and constant sacrifice.

Some people believe that good behavior should be reserved for their professional life and that they can attend to General improperly or dishonestly in their personal life.

The same morals are expected in all contexts: personal, family, and professional.

Any ethical mistakes we make will follow us for the rest of our lives, even though we may have forgotten them.

Ethical people can be very easily recognized because they know how to say no to the temptations of "elastic morality", even at the risk of losing their position, additional profits, or a business deal.

Ethics is the key to success; without it we do not deserve anyone's trust, so it will always be relevant and 'in vogue'. If we do not have a clean and honest brand, we will not be successful.

LEE HECHT HARRISON   DBM   Author: Inna Semple / Design: Hashtag

THIRTEEN
PRACTICAL IDEAS ABOUT JOBS

All jobs are temporary. They are never secure.

1

2

A job is not a right. We have to earn it every day.

Excellent performance or a high degree of loyalty does not guarantee a secure job.

3

6

A good attitude is crucial at work. The desire to learn compensates even for lack of experience.

5

It is a bad idea to continue at a job that gives us no satisfaction, because that affects our attitude and performance. Changing jobs is never easy, but not trying to do so is "professional suicide".

Many years in the same job requires that we focus even more on our performance and relevance.

4

We are paid to add quantifiable value, not for just showing up at work.

7

8

It is important to recognize ourselves as professional service providers, responsible for the quality of those services.

9

What our boss thinks of us will affect our career greatly, even many years down the road.

12

Developing our career as if it were our own best business does miracles for our employability.

11

When we resign (or we are let go) from a position, it is vital to do the job well up to the last minute.

Complacency and arrogance damage a career; improper and unethical conduct destroy it.

10

13

Taking care of our personal brand always pays off well.

LEE HECHT HARRISON **DBM**

Author: Ines Temple / Design: Hashtag

172

WHAT PROGRESS

— HAVE YOU MADE IN YOUR —

CAREER PLAN?

Making a plan starts by sitting down and thinking
what do I want to do?
where do I want to go?

It's about reflecting on everything that aligns us and gets us into shape to achieve our life and career goals.

WE OFTEN do not set career goals for ourselves, expecting our employers to promote and recognize us based on our merits.

We ourselves have to care for and take control of our career, our own employability, our own profile.

MOST PEOPLE do not develop a career life plan. They simply live without planning too much, without asking much from life, without expecting much from their careers.

This stops them from advancing, makes them become inactive, often indefinitely. It's like building a house without drawing a blueprint first.

WHENEVER I have the chance to meet successful people, I ask them: **what strategies did you use or what is your secret? How did you do it?** They mention their personal ambitions, what they expect from themselves and life, and how they see themselves in the future.

This shapes a life or career plan that they write down.
These are always flexible plans that they keep adjusting, because often things don't turn out as expected.

MAKING A CAREER PLAN is not that complicated. It takes a couple of hours to think about it and write it down. Then, we need to review and assess it two or three times a year.

But having a career plan often makes the essential competitive difference for our professional career, and it certainly greatly enhances our chances of success.

THE CHALLENGE, once our career plan is ready, is to implement it, carry it out, and believe in it.

LEE HECHT HARRISON | DBM

Author: Ines Temple / Design: Hashtag

The Power of Gratitude

In many cultures, giving thanks is deemed good manners and politeness. Some of us simply do not have the good habit of acknowledging and thanking others for their hospitality or favors. Below are some tips to keep in mind when thanks are in order.

SEND A THANK YOU E-MAIL:

Sending an e-mail after a meeting with a contact is a common practice in many cultures. We should follow their example.

VALUE THE EFFORT:

When we are thanked for a job well done, we feel valued and recognized. We appreciate that very necessary emotional salary, especially if the recognition is timely, personal, and given in the right measure.

JOB APPRECIATION AND RECOGNITION:

Though very important and necessary, they are too scarce in the work place. For example, 79 percent of the talent that resigns does so because of a lack of recognition.

WHAT COULD WE THANK MORE OR BETTER?

Favors we ask, advice we receive, information we are given, time spent on us, meetings we request, and thoughtful gestures.

Taking the time to thank, value, and recognize what others do for us is a very clear and positive way of showing them our respect and appreciation. Thanking them makes both sides feel great and always strengthens the relationship.
That is the true power of gratitude!

LEE HECHT HARRISON DBM

Author: Ines Temple / Design: Hashtag

ELEVEN REASONS
WHY YOU WILL BE FIRED

1 If **you do not add value to your organization**, if the results of your work are not easily quantifiable or measurable, or if you always have excuses for not meeting deadlines.

2 If **you are not committed** to the common purpose of the organization. Commitment, including loyalty, is essential for being successful at work.

3 If you "defend yourself" from changes and innovative ideas, and sabotage new initiatives to defend "how we have always done things here" instead, or if **your lack of excitement for innovating, changing, or improving is** evident.

4 If **you frequently quarrel** with the people you work with (even clients), if you constantly fight with everyone and make no effort to control your bad temper.

5 If **you are indiscreet or disclose confidential information** that can damage the organization, its people, or its services. If you are unable to keep a secret or if you disclose what happens behind office doors.

6 If **you are disloyal.** Disloyalty is perhaps the most powerful reason to stop trusting someone, short of extremes such as stealing, lying, or cheating; it has to do with watching out for the organization's interests.

7 If **you speak ill of your boss**, other people in the organization, or the company itself, even "only to your friends". If you are unhappy at work, you can always leave, with dignity and class.

8 If **you are unsupportive** of team efforts, or are the one who "drops everything" exactly at the end of office hours, even though everybody else is doing their part to meet a common goal or objective.

9 If **you are conceited,** belittle your boss or your colleagues, try to manipulate them, or are disrespectful to them, while complaining about everything and your bad luck at work, you would get fired for certain, and with no recommendations.

10 If **you try to cover up your mistakes** and go to great lengths to hide them without accepting your responsibility for them, even blaming others.

11 And if **your personal or financial life is a mess**, chaotic, or takes away your energy, affecting the quality of your work, you should know that you will not be spared.

LEE HECHT HARRISON DBM

Author: Ines Temple / Design: Hashtag

175

WHAT SHOULD WE DO BEFORE A JOB INTERVIEW?

The most important thing to do for a job interview is prepare:

01 Know where to go.
Go a few days earlier to know how to get there and what clothing is appropriate.

02

Research the company thoroughly. Review its website; look up the interviewer in Google, LinkedIn, or Facebook.

03

Have a clear idea of what you can contribute to the organization through the position they are offering. Bringing ideas shows interest: know what can be done and what you expect from the organization.

04

Rehearse typical interview questions, but without memorizing the answers. Film yourself to study your postures and gestures.

05

Smile as you speak: this helps to make it easier to establish a relationship of trust with the interviewer. Strive not only to be liked, but to establish a relationship of trust.

LEE HECHT HARRISON | DBM

Author: Ines Temple / Design: Hashtag

11 WAYS TO INSPIRE

1 I am inspired by people who are enthusiastic about their work, their life, or their family, and who transmit that enthusiasm and good energy to me.

2 I am inspired by people who can point out possibilities for me or my future that I had considered, that I had thought were unattainable, or that I never dared to dream of or hope for.

3 I am very inspired when people have faith in my ability to learn, to change, and to improve!

4 I am very inspired by anyone who can transmit an optimistic view of the future that makes sense to me.

5 I am very inspired by people who see the best in me, and focus on that when working with me.

6 I am inspired when problems are transparently presented to me, emphasizing possible solutions, and, above all, letting me know what is expected of me.

7 I am inspired by serious people with values, who do not lie, do not try to deceive me, and do not use me for their own ends or to cover up their mistakes.

8 I am inspired by people who celebrate the successes of others with joy and happiness, demonstrating their own strength and greatness of spirit.

9 I am inspired when people who drive change explain to me, step by step, patiently, and in advance, how these changes will affect or benefit me.

10 I am inspired by the leader or boss who is able to show his or her vulnerability upfront, because that lets me identify with him or her immediately.

11 I am inspired by people who know where they are going, who joyfully strive to accomplish their goals, and who are determined to accomplish what they set out to do and do it with enthusiasm and excitement.

LEE HECHT HARRISON | DBM

Author: Ines Temple / Design: Hashtag

MY BOSS AND I

To stand out at work, the relationship between your boss and you is as important as the company infrastructure or the passion you put into your work.

Align expectations:

Have a good understanding of what your boss expects you to do. If your boss does not take the initiative to talk with you, seek her out yourself to avoid misunderstandings.

Communicate:

Ask your boss what she expects from you. This will help you to know what you have to do and how to do it properly.

A relationship based on respect is key:

Do not underestimate her capabilities, or express your differences through attitudes, gestures, or looks.

Propose solutions:

You will earn her trust by supporting her, demonstrating that you want to help make a better organization.

Be empathetic with her:

Be attentive to her, because she probably bears a heavier burden of responsibilities than you. Be careful not to fawn on her though.

Avoid speaking ill of her:

Criticizing her in front of others, even in private or with close friends, is a serious mistake.

Determine if it is the wrong place for you:

If you feel that after all your efforts, your boss acts improperly or unethically, the best thing to do is leave that environment and try to find a new position.

LEE HECHT HARRISON | DBM

Author: Ines Temple / Design: Hashtag

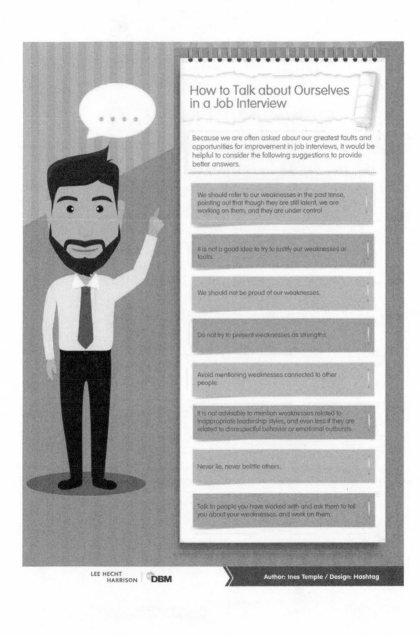

How to Talk about Ourselves in a Job Interview

Because we are often asked about our greatest faults and opportunities for improvement in job interviews, it would be helpful to consider the following suggestions to provide better answers.

We should refer to our weaknesses in the past tense, pointing out that though they are still latent, we are working on them, and they are under control.

It is not a good idea to try to justify our weaknesses or faults.

We should not be proud of our weaknesses.

Do not try to present weaknesses as strengths.

Avoid mentioning weaknesses connected to other people.

It is not advisable to mention weaknesses related to inappropriate leadership styles, and even less if they are related to disrespectful behavior or emotional outbursts.

Never lie, never belittle others.

Talk to people you have worked with and ask them to tell you about your weaknesses, and work on them.

LEE HECHT HARRISON | DBM

Author: Ines Temple / Design: Hashtag

179

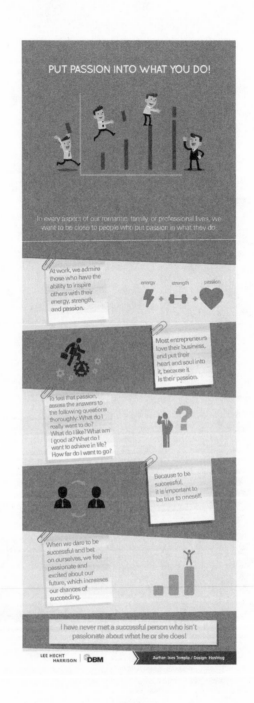

7 REASONS TO WORK WITH
PASSION

1.- RESULTS
Those who put their heart and soul into what they do are more successful; award-winning athletes, entrepreneurs, hard-fighting dreamers, and outstanding professionals give their work their utmost.

2.- SATISFACTION
The higher the cost, the greater the reward. Pushing ourselves to the maximum and accomplishing what we set out to do gives us an adrenaline rush and an incomparable feeling.

3.- COMPETITIVENESS
In a world as competitive as ours, working with passion is almost a requirement. In the working world there are many determined, innovative, and ambitious people hungering for success, so standing out is essential to achieve our goals.

4.- ENERGY
When we work intensely, we move, inspire, motivate, and stimulate others to give their best, thereby achieving the best team results.

5.- INTERNATIONAL LEVEL
Today's quality standards in the international market are highly demanding; strict contract compliance and tighter deadlines and conditions require that we give our best.

6.- REPUTATION
A good professional reputation starts with word of mouth. This results in more business and attracts more clients. Nothing has more impact than working with excellence, delivering outstanding results, and adding value.

7.- RESPONSIBILITY
Taking responsibility for doing a good job makes us put aside excuses, apathy, lethargy, sluggishness, grudges, and complexes since these do not lead to anything or produce anything good or positive. Discipline and responsibility are vital for us to rise and stand out above the rest.

LEE HECHT HARRISON | DBM

Author: Ines Temple / Design: Hashtag

NINE WAYS TO APPEAR YOUNGER

We live in a world fascinated by youth and everything it represents. The job market is no stranger to this fascination. We associate youth with a series of traits we all wish to have and maintain.

What are the attitudes or behaviors that can make us feel and appear younger?

1 Decide not to fall behind, especially in technology, science, and innovation.

2 Challenge yourselves intellectually, take different courses in "difficult" subjects, obtain new academic degrees, learn to write code or to speak a new language.

3 Increase your vitality with determination, time investment, much discipline, and personal effort.

4 Stretch your mind towards new ideas and all kinds of paradigms, especially those related to innovative ideas.

5 Cultivate curiosity and the excitement of having many new and different projects, careers, and interests. This helps us to enjoy life more, just as travelling, going out, seeing, and feeling new things do.

6 Challenge conventionalisms, being young is a mental attitude sustained by continuously rebelling against the status quo.

7 Keep away from negative, gossipy, and troublemaking people who only try to hide their unhappiness and pettiness by poisoning other people's lives.

8 Make new friends, and the more diverse and different they are from us, the better. They offer different ideas and other perspectives that refresh and renew us.

9 Visualize how you celebrate when you fulfill your goals and dreams in order to program your brain for success. This is key to achieving your goals.

Life is short; there is no time to lose!

LEE HECHT HARRISON DBM Author: Ines Temple / Design: Hashtag

ENDNOTES

Introduction

1. Lee Hecht Harrison Peru, "Reporte de Resultados: Outplacement 2017" (Results Report: Outplacement 2017) (April 2018): 3, http://lhh.pe/site/wp-content/uploads/2018/05/REPORTE -RESUL.-2017-LHH-DBM_-DIGITAL-por-PAGINAS -FINAL.pdf.
2. Ibid.; "Active Placement," Lee Hecht Harrison, www.lhh.com/our -services/career-transition-and-outplacement/ active-placement.

Chapter 1

3. World Economic Forum, *The Future of Jobs: Employment, Skills and Workforce Strategy for the Fourth Industrial Revolution* (Geneva: World Economic Forum, 2016), 13.
4. Ibid., 13-14.
5. Helen Barrett, "Plan for Five Careers in a Lifetime", *Financial Times*, September 4, 2017, FT Guides; Alison Doyle, "How Often Do People Change Jobs?", *The Balance Careers*, January 24, 2018.
6. Bureau of Labor Statistics, "Employee Tenure Summary," September 22, 2016, http://www.bls.gov/news.release/tenure. nr0.htm; "Workers Are Not Switching Jobs More Often," *The Economist*, October 21, 2017, Finance and Economics, https://

www.economist.com/finance-and-economics/2017/10/21/
workers-are-not-switching-jobs-more-often.

7. "Total Number of Employed Persons in Canada in 2017, By Job Tenure (in 1,000)," *Statista*, 2018, https://www150.statcan .gc.ca/t1/tbl1/en/tv.action?pid=1410005501.

8. "Workforce Trends 2017," *Third Sector*, May 25, 2017, https:// thirdsector.com.au/107966-2/.

9. Lee Hecht Harrison Peru, "Reporte de Resultados: Outplacement 2017" (Results Report: Outplacement 2017) (April 2018):7, http:// lhh.pe/site/wp-content/uploads/2018/05/REPORTE-RESUL .-2017-LHH-DBM_-DIGITAL-por-PAGINAS-FINAL.pdf

10. Ibid., 3.

11. The Japan Institute for Labor Policy and Training, "Labor Situation in Japan and Its Analysis: General Overview 2015/2016," Series Archive, 74-76, June 21, 2018, http://www.jil.go.jp/english/lsj/ general/2015-2016/2015-2016.pdf

Chapter 3

12. Jack Welch and Suzy Welch, *Winning* (New York: Harper Collins, 2005).

13. Remarks made by Jack Welch at a presentation transmitted to several countries simultaneously many years ago. Panels were formed in each country to discuss his presentation, and I was a panel member here in Peru. His words stuck with me, but I'm afraid I forget when this presentation and panel took place.

14. Amy Rees Anderson, "What It Takes To Be A Great Employee: The Parable Of The Oranges," *Forbes*, May 22, 2016, https:// www.forbes.com/sites/amyanderson/2016/05/22/what-it -takes-to-be-a-great-employee-the-parable-of-the-oranges/.

Chapter 4

15. Glyn Philip Morris, "The power of written goals – Part 1," Mind Health Development, November 27, 2017, last visited June 1, 2018, https://mindhealthdevelopment.com/2017/11/27/the-power-of-written-goals-part-1/.

16. Dr. Gail Matthews, "Goals Research Summary," https://www.dominican.edu/academics/lae/undergraduate-programs/psych/faculty/assets-gail-matthews/researchsummary2.pdf.

17. Dominican University of California, "Study Focuses on Strategies for Achieving Goals, Resolutions," January 5, 2017, News, Room, last visited May 31, 2018, https://www.dominican.edu/dominicannews/study-highlights-strategies-for-achieving-goals.

18. Mark Murphy, Neuroscience Explains Why You Need To Write Down Your Goals If You Actually Want To Achieve Them, Forbes, April 15, 2018, last visited May 31, 2018, https://www.forbes.com/sites/markmurphy/2018/04/15/neuroscience-explains-why-you-need-to-write-down-your-goals-if-you-actually-want-to-achieve-them/#1dcfa4d27905.

19. Stephen Covey, The 7 Habits of Highly Effective People (New York: Simon & Schuster, 1990), 97-99.

Chapter 5

20. Dave Munger, "The Six-Second Teacher Evaluator," Science Blog, May 1, 2006, http://scienceblogs.com/cognitivedaily/2006/05/01/the-sixsecond-teacher-evaluati/; N. Ambady and R. Rosenthal, "Half a Minute: Predicting Teacher Evaluations from Thin Slices of Nonverbal Behavior and Physical Attractiveness," Journal of Personality and Social Psychology 64, no. 3 (1993): 431-441.

21. Simon Holliday, "Spread the Word: What Mehrabian Really Tells Us about Communication," LinkedIn, January 19, 2015,

https://www.linkedin.com/pulse/spread-word-what-mehrabian-really-tells-us-simon-holliday/.

22. Lee Hecht Harrison Peru DBM, "Resultados de Encuesta Sobre Redes Sociales 2014" (Results of Social Networks Survey), Publicaciones, 31 December 2014, 13, http://lhh.pe/site/wp-content/uploads/2014/12/Informe-Estudio-Redes-Sociales-2014.pdf.

23. Keith Ferrazzi, *Never Eat Alone: And Other Secrets to Success, One Relationship at a Time* (New York: Currency, 2005), 298.

24. Ibid., 149.

25. Jack Welch and Suzy Welch, *Winning* (New York: Harper Collins, 2005).

26. Herminia Ibarra, *Working Identity: Unconventional Strategies for Reinventing Your Career* (Massachusetts: Harvard Business School Publishing, 2004).

27. Jeffrey Gitomer, *Little Black Book of Connections: 6.5 Assets for Networking Your Way to Rich Relationships* (Texas: Bard Press, 2006).

28. Gina Belli, "How Many Jobs are Found Through Networking, Really?", *PayScale*, April 6, 2017, https://www.payscale.com/career-news/2017/04/many-jobs-found-networking.

29. Lou Adler, "New Survey Reveals 85% of All Jobs are Filled Via Networking," *LinkedIn*, February 29, 2016, https://www.linkedin.com/pulse/new-survey-reveals-85-all-jobs-filled-via-networking-lou-adler.

30. Lee Hecht Harrison Peru DBM, "Resultados de Encuesta Sobre Redes Sociales 2014" (Results of Social Networks Survey), Publicaciones, 31 December 2014, http://lhh.pe/site/wp-content/uploads/2014/12/Informe-Estudio-Redes-Sociales-2014.pdf.

31. Ibid., 6.

32. Ibid., 7.

33. Ibid.

34. Ibid., 11.

35. Ibid., 12.

36. Ibid., 12.